PERSONAL
POWER ANIMALS
For Guidance, Protection and Healing

Madonna Gauding

A GODSFIELD BOOK
www.godsfieldpress.com

First published in Great Britain in 2006
by Godsfield Press,
a division of Octopus Publishing Group Ltd
2–4 Heron Quays,
London, E14 4JP

Distributed in the United States and Canada by
Sterling Publishing Co, Inc.
387 Park Avenue South, New York, NY 10016–8810

ISBN-13: 978-1-84181-292-2

ISBN-10: 1-84181-292-7

A CIP catalogue record for this book
is available from the British Library

10 9 8 7 6 5 4 3 2 1

Printed and bound in China

CONTENTS

INTRODUCTION

WHAT IS A POWER ANIMAL?

If you have never heard of power animals, you have come to the right place. This book will teach you about power animals – what they are, how to identify them and how to access their spiritual power for healing, personal growth, protection and guidance.

Because we live in modern times, many of us have lost our connection with nature, animals and the spirit world. So, to help us understand what personal power animals are, we need to backtrack in time, when a different mindset prevailed, one that might actually help us to heal ourselves and our world today.

IN TOUCH WITH THE UNIVERSE

Long ago, our ancestors experienced all things as alive, animated and filled with soul.

They experienced themselves as part of this great, interconnected web of life. For them, trees, stars, stones, personal objects and all living beings – from the lowly ant to the majestic elephant – embodied sacred consciousness. Their universe was a sacred one, alive with signs, messages and omens, which they perceived as manifestations of divine wisdom and guidance. In this enlivened, interconnected world, animals were considered to be teachers and carriers of those messages.

If you are sceptical about the existence of power animals, remember that our collective mythology and sacred scripture are populated with angels, ghosts, fairies, elves and animal spirits. And, despite our contemporary, scientific, rational minds, our hearts have not really lost faith in that enchanted, spirit-filled world. For example, the hugely successful *Harry Potter* fantasy book series, which includes many magical power animals, has sold millions of copies worldwide and been translated into 60 languages. So, while reading this book, pay attention to that pull at your heart and try giving our ancestors the benefit of the doubt. After all, how could so many of our relatives, in so many cultures, through so many millennia, be so wrong?

THE POWER WITHIN

A power animal is an internal helper, companion and guide, in the form of a natural or magical animal, which possesses qualities you need in this world. You may already possess those qualities, yet they are dormant within you, or you may need to develop them. Your power animal helps you access higher wisdom, either your own or that of a higher power. It also helps you heal from emotional or physical illness, acts as your guardian and protector and functions as your oracle bringing you messages from the divine.

Don't be disappointed if you discover you have a seemingly insignificant, non-threatening power animal, such as a mouse, frog or insect. As you will learn, all power animals, whether natural or magical, are special beings and possess extraordinary skills and qualities, including the ability to shape-shift into larger size. Trust that the power animal you identify will be the one you need at this particular time in your life.

THE HUMAN–ANIMAL CONNECTION

Until recent times, humans dwelled alongside animals in a world believed to be a manifestation of the divine. Within this sacred context, they relied on animals for food, clothing, shelter and companionship. Early cave paintings at Lascaux and Trois Frères in France, dating from around 15,000 BCE, depict magical images of horses and bulls, drawn both to appease and to capture the animal's spirit. Sheep, goats and cattle were first domesticated around 6000 BCE. Around that time, in the Middle East, images of the Great Mother goddess and her sacred animals began to appear. She was worshipped in the various form of the bird, cow, pig and serpent.

Throughout the world, from Siberia to the African continent, from Europe to the Americas, indigenous tribes and clans identified themselves with special animal totems. Their holy men and women, or shamans, transformed themselves into animal form through altered states of consciousness and, by doing this, accessed their wisdom, guidance and protection. Animals were considered helpers and messengers of the divine.

WHEN THINGS BEGAN TO CHANGE

Up until recent history, we continued to live in agrarian cultures, in close proximity to wild and domesticated animals. Beginning in the 19th century, the sacred, natural, spirited world gave way to the urban, industrial age and its rational, scientific viewpoint. Our special relationship with animals suffered in the transition. Having your own personal power animal will help you manifest the sacred human–animal connection in your own life.

WHY HAVE A RELATIONSHIP WITH A POWER ANIMAL?

Working with power animals reintroduces you to the natural world. If nature once delighted you when you were a child, you may feel that you are coming home to a part of yourself you once lost. Through the process of discovering your power animal, you will think about, learn about and perhaps be with animals you have never thought about before. Even your back yard will take on a new fascination, as you become attuned to the veritable menagerie of birds, animals, reptiles and insects that call it home.

MAKING CONNECTIONS

As you begin the journey of discovering your own power animal, you will be reminded that you inhabit a vast, interconnected universe. This profound realization is one of the best antidotes to depression and alienation – the kind that can come from thinking of yourself as alone and separate from everyone and everything else.

On an energetic level, everything *is* interconnected. Modern physics confirms this, as do the ancient wisdom traditions of the world. When you next look at that awesome tiger in the zoo or safari park, or on the television, a chill will go up your spine knowing you are deeply connected to and a part of, that beauty and power. You will learn that tiger energy resides in you and, if you want, you can develop tiger's qualities and make use of his unique gifts.

POSITIVE ENERGY

As you explore animals as spirit guides, you will begin to work with energy on a non-physical level. You will find that your mind, your intention, your prayers and visualizations create energy that affects you and the rest of the universe. As you work with your power animal, you have the opportunity to create positive energy that will enhance your life and that of those around you.

DISCOVER THE SACRED

Power animals not only bring you closer to nature and help you understand the energetic interdependence of all living and non-living things, they introduce you to the world as a manifestation of the sacred. When you accept that divine spirit flows through all reality – even that annoying mole in your garden – your life is transformed. When you regard everything and everyone, including yourself, as sacred, you will find it easier to extend your compassion – toward yourself, your friends and family, your co-workers, your enemies, strangers and, of course, your brothers and sisters of the animal world.

BENEFITS

By working with power animals, through meditation, visualization and direct contact, you will access the animal's unique wisdom. You will be able to ask your power animal for advice, guidance, protection and healing – and your power animal will be there for you. If you have an illness or injury, your power animal can help you recover. Finally, you will learn about your own animal nature. When you access this repressed side of yourself, you enrich your life and paradoxically become more fully human.

Kundalini – referred to throughout the book – is a psychospiritual energy that resides dormant within the body and is aroused through yoga or some other spiritual discipline to cause heightened states of physical and mental consciousness, including mystical illumination or enlightenment. The word kundalini is Sanskrit for 'snake' or 'serpent power', because it is believed the energy lies like a serpent in the root chakra at the base of the spine.

HOW TO USE THIS BOOK

You may be tempted to go straight to the 'Power Animals Directory' and choose your power animal according to which you like best. As you will learn, this is not how it works.

INTRODUCTORY SECTIONS AND EXERCISES

It is important to read through the beginning sections of this book in their entirety and complete the exercises prepared for you. In this way, you will deepen your understanding of animal spirit guides and learn the proper way to identify your personal power animal and work with its energies.

THE DIRECTORY

Consult the Directory as instructed in the exercises, and use it as a starting point to understand both yourself and your power animal or animals. Over time, you may have more than one. The Directory is divided into earth element, water element, air element and magical animals. Each entry includes the animal's myths and stories and the person you are (or could be) if this is your power animal. It may describe both your positive and negative qualities, along with unique ways your power animal can help you and methods for accessing its power. In addition, you will find information on the animal as a dream symbol, as a guardian or protector, as a healer, and its possible meaning as an oracle or omen.

KEEP A JOURNAL

If possible, create a special journal for documenting your relationship with your power animal.

POWER ANIMALS AROUND THE WORLD

ANIMAL TOTEMS

A totem is an animal or a natural object that serves as the emblem of an indigenous tribal clan and speaks of the tribe's mystical connection with animals and the natural world. The totem animal was the tribe's guardian and protector and was sometimes considered the tribe's ancestor. Clan members believed in their special relationship with the animal or animals and would strive to emulate their qualities. When representing an individual, the term 'totem animal' and 'power animal' are interchangeable. In other words, a power animal can also be called your totem animal.

TOTEM POLES

Many Native American tribes, particularly those of the Pacific Northwest, carved the clan's emblems on totem poles. The totem pole was carved from a large tree trunk and depicted animal totems – animal characters and sacred objects from the tribe's stories and myths. The carved figures were painted with natural pigments and decorated with feathers, beaks, claws and other ornaments. When the totem pole was raised the tribe members would hold a 'potlatch' or feast. One totem pole preserved in Canada shows symbols of the moon, a goat, human faces of the people who created the carving, a bear and a whale. These animals had great significance and meaning for the tribe. Some tribes, like the Delaware, Iroquois and Shawnee, world erect totem poles inside their houses.

Other aboriginal people around the world had similar creations. The Maori people of New Zealand constructed totem poles to celebrate their ancestors, and the Ainu of Japan created groupings of totem poles as playgrounds for their gods.

CELTIC TOTEMS

The Celts, an ancient European people who emerged around 1500 BCE, had profound relationships with their animal totems. Many Celtic artefacts are decorated with totem animals that identified their various tribes or clans. Their shamans, who had the ability to contact deceased ancestors and foretell the future, would enlist the aid of the clan's totem animals to help them in their role as healers and visionaries.

Each animal possessed unique virtues and qualities and had its own peculiar powers and would be called on as needed. The shaman entered an altered state and adopt the shape and consciousness of the chosen totem animal. By entering this altered state, the shaman would take on its qualities and abilities – the strength of the bear, the speed of the horse, the keen eyesight of the hawk. He or she would then bring the perspective and skills of the totem animal to bear in solving the problem at hand.

MODERN EXAMPLES

The practice of adopting totem animals continues to this day in the naming of American sports teams, such as the Chicago Bulls or Detroit Lions. Contemporary European/American surnames recall clan totems of the past, such as 'Leonard' from the Norman meaning 'lion brave' and 'Phillips', which is Greek for 'horse lover'.

ANIMAL GODS AND GODDESSES

The sacredness of the human animal connection is reflected in every ancient culture through the astonishing number of deities depicted in animal form. Deities were envisioned as animals, as half-human and half-animal, or human accompanied by an animal emblem or totem. The following, very brief, list gives you an idea of how our ancestors perceived animals – as sources of magic and mystery, keepers of wisdom and even manifestations of the divine.

- The ancient Mimbres people of the American Southwest depicted their fertility goddess as a scorpion.
- In central India, Chamunda, a wrathful form of the goddess Durga, is also shown in scorpion form.
- Figurines from Crete, dating from Neolithic times, depict a human-bodied, bird-headed goddess. Other Cretan goddesses are in human form, yet hold powerful snakes aloft in each hand.
- In the Sahara-Atlas mountains in what is modern-day Algeria, prehistoric rock carvings, dating from 7000 BCE, show a man worshipping a goddess in the form of a sheep. The sheep is dressed regally with a necklace and a sun disk on her head.
- Archaeologists in Iran discovered a realistic statue, dating from 2900 BCE, of a kneeling cow-headed goddess who appears to be engaged in a religious ritual.
- In India, the god Vishnu is sometimes depicted as a fish. In his fish form, he is identified with the feminine moon. Sacred fish are still kept in pools in India today.
- As recently as 1850, a Zuni tribesperson in the United States created a 'kachina', or ritual doll, with a cow's head and human body.
- Until recent times, the Baga tribe of Guinea worshipped Niniganni, a goddess in python form.

ANCIENT EGYPTIAN ANIMAL DEITIES

- The baboon was one of the manifestations of Thoth, god of writing.
- Bast, the famous protector cat goddess, is shown as a cat or a human with the head of a cat. During her festival, thousands of people would travel by boat to her cult centre in Bubastis, drinking, singing and calling out dirty jokes to those on the shore.
- The god Set took the form of a pig. As a pig, he blinded the god Horus. The blinded eyes of Horus are said to represent the solar and lunar eclipses.
- Anubis, the god of mummification, is shown as a man with the head of a jackal or dog. The jackal was considered a guide for the newly dead.
- Sekhmet, another Egyptian goddess, shown as a lioness or a lioness-headed woman, was known for her healing powers.
- Hathor, Isis and Nut were three goddesses who were depicted either as cows or with a human face but the horns or ears of a cow.
- One of the most stunningly beautiful images from Egypt, dated around 4000 BCE, shows a graceful feminine divinity with a woman's torso, a bird's head and outstretched arms with exquisite feather-like hands.

ANIMALS OF THE ZODIAC

The word 'zodiac' is an ancient Greek word meaning 'circle of animals'. In Western astrology, the zodiac is a band-shaped section of the sky that contains 12 special constellations. Astrologers believe that each person is deeply influenced by the sign of the zodiac under which they were born. Each of the 12 astrological symbols indicates something about the personality of those born under that sign. Both the Western and Eastern zodiac make use of real and magical animal symbols.

WESTERN ZODIAC

The origin of the Western zodiac probably comes from our prehistoric ancestors observing that the seasons changed when certain groups of stars reached certain positions in the night sky. They remembered the constellations by naming them after the human, animal or other figures that their outline suggested. Around 2000 BCE, the Babylonians created the zodiac as a method of visuliazing the passage of time, that marked the 12 moons that appear in the year.

SIGNS OF THE WESTERN ZODIAC

Sign	Symbol	Dates	CHARACTERISTICS
Aries	Ram	21 March to 20 April	Energetic, creative, self-confident
Taurus	Bull	21 April to 21 May	Sensuous, pragmatic, strong-willed
Gemini	Twins	22 May to 21 June	Flexible, ingenious, quick-witted
Cancer	Crab	22 June to 22 July	Sensitive, intuitive, emotional
Leo	Lion	23 July to 23 August	Enthusiastic, determined, proud
Virgo	Virgin	24 August to 22 September	Wise, practical, detail-oriented
Libra	Scales	23 September to 23 October	Balanced, charming, artistic
Scorpio	Scorpion	24 October to 22 November	Mysterious, intense, inquisitive
Sagittarius	Centaur	23 November to 21 December	Idealistic, philosophical, adventurous
Capricorn	Goat	22 December to 20 January	Hard-working, logical, ambitious
Aquarius	Water-bearer	21 January to 19 February	Principled, unorthodox, intellectual
Pisces	Fish	20 February to 20 March	Compassionate, unpredictable, risk-taking

EASTERN ZODIAC

The Eastern zodiac, also called the Chinese zodiac, is a set of 12 animal symbols used since ancient times. The Eastern zodiac does not involve constellations and has no historical connection with the Western zodiac. As in the Western zodiac, it is believed that the symbol under which a person is born influences their character and fate. The Chinese zodiac matches animals to years that repeat in a 12-year cycle. The first Eastern zodiac is based on the classical philosophy of Confucius, Lao Tse and the *I Ching*. It is made up of a set of 12 animal symbols, and has been in continuous use since Emperor Huang Ti introduced it in 2637 BCE.

According to Chinese legend, the order of the 12 signs was determined by Buddha, who, during one New Year's celebration, invited all of the animals in the kingdom together for a meeting, yet only 12 creatures attended. The order of the animals in the Chinese zodiac corresponds to the order in which the animals arrived at their meeting with the Buddha.

SIGNS OF THE EASTERN ZODIAC

Sign	Years	CHARACTERISTICS
Rat	1912, 1924, 1936, 1948, 1960, 1972, 1984, 1996	Charming, successful, perfectionist
Ox	1913, 1925, 1937, 1949, 1961, 1973, 1985, 1997	Patient, easy-going, eloquent
Tiger	1914, 1926, 1938, 1950, 1962, 1974, 1986, 1998	Sensitive, short-tempered, thoughtful
Rabbit	1915, 1927, 1939, 1951, 1963, 1975, 1987, 1999	Articulate, virtuous, clever
Dragon	1916, 1928, 1940, 1952, 1964, 1976, 1988, 2000	Energetic, brave, eccentric
Snake	1917, 1929, 1941, 1953, 1965, 1977, 1989, 2001	Wise, sympathetic, determined
Horse	1918, 1930, 1942, 1954, 1966, 1978, 1990, 2002	Cheerful, perceptive, impatient
Ram	1919, 1931, 1943, 1955, 1967, 1979, 1991, 2003	Elegant, artistic, passionate
Monkey	1920, 1932, 1944, 1956, 1968, 1980, 1992, 2004	Erratic, brilliant, skilful
Rooster	1921, 1933, 1945, 1957, 1969, 1981, 1993, 2005	Capable, devoted, talented
Dog	1922, 1934, 1946, 1958, 1970, 1982, 1994, 2006	Loyal, honest, discreet
Pig	1923, 1935, 1947, 1959, 1971, 1983, 1995, 2007	Chivalrous, scholarly, kind

ANIMALS IN MYTH, FABLE AND FAIRYTALE

All world cultures have stories about animals or animals as human characters. Aesop's fables from ancient Greece, the Jataka tales from Buddhist scripture, Grimm's fairytales from the European tradition and Native American coyote tales are but a few examples of animal stories used to impart knowledge and pass down wisdom to the next generation.

AESOP'S FABLES

Some of the most beloved animal stories are those attributed to a Greek slave named Aesop, who died around 565 BCE. In Aesop's lifetime, two different masters owned him, and the second, named Iadmon, gave him his freedom as a reward for his great wit and extraordinary intelligence. His stories have stood the test of time and were among the first secular printed works in European languages. Like all fables, each of his tales eaches a moral lesson. In most of Aesop's tales, the animal characters talk and act like humans, and through their voices he reveals our failings and virtues with compassion and humour. Each of his fables ends with a proverb that sums up the story's moral and advice.

One of the most popular of Aesop's fables is about a tortoise and hare who agree to race. Halfway through the race, the hare is so far ahead and confident of winning that he stops to nap. Of course, the tortoise plods along and passes him. The hare awakens to see the tortoise cross the finish line. The moral is 'slow and steady wins the race', which teaches that persistence can deliver success.

JATAKA TALES

Another hare story appears in the Jataka tales, the ancient Buddhist animal fables recorded over several centuries from 300 BCE to AD 400. This collection of 550 stories tells of the earlier incarnations of Siddhartha Gautama, the person who would later become Buddha Shakyamuni.

As the story goes, in one of his previous births the Buddha was born as a hare. He had three friends – a monkey, a jackal and an otter. Together they decided to practise charity on a religious feast day in order to create good karma and earn extra spiritual merit. The otter, jackal and monkey were more superstitious than religious, and quickly bought or stole their offerings. The hare could not find anything that he considered to be good enough for almsgiving, so he decided to offer his entire body to charity.

Indra, the king of the gods, did not believe the hare was sincere. So he tested the hare by disguising himself as an ascetic and chasing after him as if to kill him for food. The hare was delighted, because this provided him with an opportunity to practise his ultimate charitable act. He asked the ascetic to kindle a fire, so he could jump in and offer his roasted meat to him.

Indra caused the heap of burning coals to appear and the hare fell on the fire. The fire, however, did not burn him. Indra revealed his identity and applauded the hare's generosity by saying, 'Oh wise hare, may your virtue be known for eons!' He then placed the image of the hare on the moon for all to see.

GRIMMS' FAIRYTALES

This famous collection of European folk tales was assembled by two brothers, Jakob and Wilhelm Grimm, in the early 19th century. Many involve animals or animal characters. One of the most famous is the story of Little Red Riding Hood, a naïve little girl who is taken advantage of and eaten by a trickster wolf who disguises himself as the little girl's loving grandmother. The moral of the story is clear: children should never talk to strangers – if they do, they may end up providing dinner for a dangerous 'wolf', disguised as a charming, sweet, polite, person.

NATIVE AMERICAN COYOTE TALES

The following, somewhat gruesome, tale is about the coyote as creator. Before people inhabited the earth, a monster walked upon the land, eating all the animals except Coyote. Realizing that Coyote was sly and clever, the monster invited him to stay in his home. When he got there, Coyote asked if he could enter the monster's stomach to visit his friends. The monster allowed this and Coyote cut out its heart, set fire to its insides and freed his friends.

Then Coyote flung pieces of the monster in the four directions, and wherever the pieces landed a new tribe of Native Americans emerged. Because he ran out of body parts, he used the monster's blood on his hands to create the fifth tribe.

SACRED ANIMALS

In some religious traditions, certain animals are considered particularly sacred.

THE COW

In Hinduism, the cow is believed to be a treasure produced from the cosmic ocean by the gods. The five products of the cow – milk, curd, butter, urine and dung – are said to be purifying and healing when mixed together. Because cows are still considered sacred in India today, they are given the freedom to wander wherever they choose. Their horns are often decorated with flowers and coloured ornaments, as a sign of respect and affection.

THE LAMB

In the Christian tradition, the lamb is an ancient and universal symbol of Christ. The Easter lamb, depicted with a halo and the flag of victory, is a popular image found in the homes of many contemporary Eastern European Catholic families. The Paschal lamb represents Christ as the lamb of sacrifice, whose blood redeemed all people. The image is drawn from the Bible, in the Book of Revelation (5:12): 'Worthy is the Lamb that was slain to receive power and riches, wisdom and strength, honour and glory and praise!'

THE DOVE

In the Old Testament of the Bible, a dove released from Noah's ark returned with an olive branch to show that the flood was over. Because of this biblical reference, the dove continues to symbolize deliverance and peace, worldwide. In Christianity, the Holy Ghost of the Trinity is often portrayed as a dove. According to European legend, the devil can turn himself into any bird except the dove.

FINDING YOUR PERSONAL POWER ANIMAL

ANIMALS THAT ATTRACT AND REPEL YOU

Although you may think you choose your power animal, actually your power animal chooses you. In fact, you may already have one or more power animals. Some indigenous peoples say that you are born with two or three power animals that function as your protectors. When you learn to work with them, they may take on many other roles – these could be as guide, teacher or healer.

The power animal you identify could be one that has already been with you, or it could be a new one that you need at this time. Consciously identifying and working with your power animal, whether old or new, will train you to work with other power animals as you need them. Finding your power animal is a process that takes place over time. The exercises in this book will help you begin that process and teach you how to develop a living relationship with your power animal.

LEARNING FROM YOUR RESPONSE

A power animal's wisdom is transmitted through its gifts and qualities, which it helps you embody in your own life. It also can function as a messenger delivering wisdom and guidance from your higher power. The purpose of this exercise is for you to learn that a strong positive or negative response could be a sign that an animal may have much to teach you. Why would you want to work with a power animal that once repelled you? That animal may be the perfect guide to help you discover hidden strengths. It may help you overcome obstacles to realizing your own power. It could help you heal deep wounds.

When you do the remaining exercises, keep your mind and heart open for whatever animal emerges. Try to put your ego aside and allow your power animal to show itself to you.

Let's begin by exploring your past and present relationship to animals. Gather your power animal journal and your favourite pen, find a little quiet time and complete the following exercise.

IDENTIFYING ANIMALS THAT ATTRACT AND REPEL ME

1 Remember the last time you visited a zoo or safari park. Which animals did you really want to see? Which animals fascinated you most and why?

2 Which animals intrigued you as a child? Did you have a special interest in the bear, the horse, the rabbit or the hippopotamus? Which animals fired your imagination?

3 List any other animals that elicit an emotional excitement when you think about them or see them. Why is that?

4 Now, list any animal the very thought of which makes you recoil and evokes revulsion. This animal may make your skin crawl. What about them provokes this response in you?

5 Which animals frightens you and why? Did you have a traumatic experience with an animal in the past?

IDENTIFYING YOUR POWER ANIMAL

The following exercise for identifying your power animal asks you to engage your imagination. Why? By creating mental images, you bypass your controlling ego and open yourself to experiences beyond literal, everyday reality. It is in imaginative space that you and your power animal will really connect and communicate. It is only through being open to and participating in ongoing imaginative processes that you will start to receive the many gifts and blessings of your power animal.

MEETING YOUR POWER ANIMAL

Gather your journal or a pad of paper and have it near for recording your thoughts and emotions after the exercise is complete. Find a quiet place where you can sit or lie down, while keeping your spine straight. Take the telephone off the hook and make sure you will not be interrupted. Make yourself as comfortable as possible. Read the exercise ahead of time, or record it and play it back.

1 Begin by closing your eyes and breathing deeply. Starting at your toes, focus on each part of your body, relaxing your muscles and any tense areas as you go. Take your time as you work your way to your crown. When you feel fully relaxed, move on to the visualization that follows.

2 Imagine yourself standing in a field of wild flowers. Close by, on your right, you see a very large, old oak tree. It is immense and has an extraordinary presence. Approach it and look up at its majestic canopy. As you walk around its trunk, you discover a large hollow on one side.

Without hesitation you enter this magical space. As you step inside, you are amazed to see there are stairs leading to some place below. You are not afraid and you decide to explore where this magical staircase leads. Torches light your way and after a few minutes you reach the bottom. Before you a short tunnel leads out to a beautiful meadow. You walk through the tunnel and exit into an almost magical landscape.

3 The air is clear, the sky is blue and the clouds are white and puffy. The grass is unbelievably soft and lush. You notice a stand of pines to the left and you are drawn to it. The invigorating smell of pine needles fills the air as you enter the sacred pine grove. It is suddenly very quiet. The bright sun gives way to soft, filtered light. It is so peaceful you cannot help but want to stay. You continue walking and arrive at a large clearing with a small, crystal-clear pool. You sit down next to it on a boulder. You close your eyes. You have not felt this relaxed and peaceful in years.

4 After a long while, you take a deep breath and look around. You notice something is moving out of the corner of your eye. It could be on the ground or flying above. It could be sitting on a branch or in the clear pool. You gently turn your head and meet the eyes of an animal. When you meet the eyes of this animal, you recognize there is something familiar and fascinating about it. If you have been afraid or repulsed by it before, you are no longer. If you have never thought about it or seen it, you are delighted to be meeting it for the first time.

5 You remain motionless, eyes meeting eyes. You open your heart to this animal and begin to hear it mentally telling you how it has helped you in the past and/or how it can help you now and in the future. It is as if you can hear its thoughts. You sit in wonder, amazed at how you have been blessed to meet this beautiful natural or magical creature.

6 Knowing intuitively that your visit is coming to an end, you thank your animal for appearing to you. You ask it to help you know if it is your power animal by giving you some kind of sign during the coming weeks. It could be sighting it in real life, observing it on television, reading about it in the newspaper, dreaming about it or some other sign.

7 Your animal turns and disappears into the forest, into the pool or into the sky above. You rise and walk slowly out of the pine grove and back through the beautiful meadow. You re-enter the tunnel, climb the stairs and exit the hollow of the magnificent mother oak tree. You are in the field of wild flowers again. Take a few deep breaths and open your eyes to re-enter the room in which you started your journey. Move slowly, stretch and feel grounded in your body and in your environment. Take your time getting up.

8 In your journal, describe the animal you met, how it behaved, what it communicated and any thoughts and feelings you may have about your journey. Write down any past encounters with the animal and anything else that comes to mind.

CONSULTING THE DIRECTORY

Now it is time to study your animal by turning to the Power Animals Directory starting on page 64 (the Directory is not exhaustive, so be aware that your animal may not be listed there). Look for additional resources at your local library or on the internet. Read about the animal's special gifts and qualities. Meditate on the animal and imagine yourself forming a relationship with it. See if its special skills are what you need at this particular time in your life. Only you can confirm if this is really your power animal.

If you don't feel the animal you encountered is your power animal, then repeat the imaginative journey above. Don't become discouraged if you don't immediately identify your power animal. With patience, your power animal will find you and you will know when it has arrived.

HONOURING YOUR POWER ANIMAL

Now that you have identified and confirmed your power animal, it is important to find ways to honour your new and very special relationship. The more you honour your power animal, the more significance it will have in your life and the more you will benefit from its wisdom.

IMAGES, JEWELLERY AND CLOTHING

You will be communicating and learning from your power animal through visualization, meditation, movement and other imaginative activities. When you are not working consciously with a power animal, it helps to keep its image close at hand, to remind you of the constant presence of this wonderful being in your life. While you are washing the dishes or sitting at your desk at work, seeing an image of your power animal out of the corner of your eye can be both comforting and empowering. The image will remind you that this spirit guide is always available and will help you grow and prosper in all areas of your life.

Try cutting out photos of your animal from old magazines. Frame them, put them on your refrigerator or tack them to a bulletin board. Organizations dedicated to wildlife preservation often provide wonderful posters or calendars with high-quality photographs or drawings of birds and animals. Consider buying a small statue, figurine or fetish small enough to carry in your pocket. Keep your eyes peeled at car-boot or garage sales for statues or images of your animal. If you are artistically inclined, paint or draw your power animal in a way that pleases you.

Wearing animal jewellery is a wonderful way to affirm your relationship with your totem animal. For example, if your animal is a bear, wearing a silver bear pin or bear earrings will remind you that the bear's energy and wisdom are always accessible to you. Wearing its image helps you to embody its many wonderful qualities. Happily, today there are many artisans creating jewellery for people who work with power animals. You can find them online or at craft festivals. Also, try Native American, Celtic and African jewellery for great animal designs.

Wearing an image of your power animal on your clothing is another way to honour your relationship. However, refrain from wearing actual fur, feathers, teeth or claws. Instead, choose sweaters, jackets or T-shirts imprinted, woven or embroidered with your animal's image. Proudly wearing your animal's image on your clothes or bag is similar to traditional Native Americans displaying totem emblems on their blankets and shields. If that is too flashy for you, try a more subtle approach and simply wear your power animal's colours. For example, if your animal is a deer, you may enjoy wearing subtle tans and cream colours; if it is a butterfly, experiment with wearing very bright orange, yellows and reds.

Remember that no one has to know you have a relationship with a power animal if you want to keep it private. If you wear your animal's emblem, others may assume nothing more than you happen to like horses, birds or dragonflies. Your power animal image can be tiny and personal, large and public, hidden or displayed. It is up to you.

EDUCATING YOURSELF ABOUT YOUR POWER ANIMAL

With any new relationship, it is important to learn everything you can about the other person. In the same way, it is essential that you educate yourself about your power animal, or your power animal will have difficulty communicating with you. Ongoing study helps you understand the gifts and qualities your power animal will bring to you. Use the Power Animals Directory, the internet, the library, television nature shows and any other resources you can find. If your animal is magical, learn about its qualities and gifts through art, literature and mythology.

As an example, if your power animal is a hawk, carefully study its habitat, appearance and diet, how it cares for its young and how it moves and flies. Watch a nature video about hawks. Notice how the hawk will pounce on its prey. By understanding how the hawk feeds itself, you may learn to be more decisive and swift when opportunities arise.

In this way, the more you learn about your animal's nature, qualities and skills, the more you will understand what lessons it holds for you. Learning will help you take on your animal's perspective and understand its messages.

Whenever possible, experience your power animal in the wild. If your animal is a deer or racoon or squirrel, try to catch a glimpse of it in a park or forest area. Get to know its habitat and the other animals, plants and insects in its environment. A zoo or safari park, of course, is not a natural environment, but, if your animal is from another part of the world, being able to see it in the flesh is a blessing. You will learn much just being in its presence, even in its captive state.

DONATING TIME AND RESOURCES TO PROTECT ANIMALS

Finally, donate your time and resources to protect your power animal in its natural environment. Volunteer at a nature reserve, a wild animal shelter, a zoo or safari park, an aquarium, or a horse, dog, cat or farm animal rescue organization. If your animal is aquatic, work to clean up and protect the ocean, river or lake in which it lives. If your animal makes its home on land, work to protect its habitat. If your animal is on the endangered species list, work to save it from extinction. Working to protect animals is a way to honour your power animal and the precious, interdependent and fragile planet that we all share.

MESSAGES FROM YOUR POWER ANIMAL

You must connect and communicate with your power animal in order to receive its messages. Your imagination is the key to learning what your power animal has to teach you and the bridge for applying its wisdom to your everyday life.

Try the following exercise to help you establish your relationship with your power animal and to work through any resistance you may have to hearing what it may have to say. Remember, the more you learn about your power animal, through extensive study, understanding and appreciation of its qualities and gifts, the more powerful and beneficial your relationship will become. As in human encounters, you appreciate and value advice from someone you both know and respect.

LEARNING TO RECEIVE AND ACCEPT MESSAGES

In order to benefit from your relationship with your power animal, you must be receptive to its messages, which may be positive, challenging, humorous, playful or profound. If you have felt emotionally guarded, cynical and disappointed in life, this exercise will prepare you to open your heart to accept the gifts, the support and the teachings your power animal has to offer.

1 Find time to be alone, sit quietly with your eyes closed and breathe deeply until relaxed.

2 Imagine your power animal sitting in front of you. Ask your power animal to identify one of your gifts and give you an example of how you manifest it in your life. For example, it may tell you that you are kind-hearted and remind you of a time when you made yourself available to a friend who was going through a divorce. Or it may tell you that you are very intelligent and give you an example of how you solved a difficult problem using your analytical skills.

3 Breathe in deeply three times, and fully accept and validate whatever your power animal tells you. Acknowledge that you have this particular skill or quality or gift, and ask your power animal to show you ways in the coming days how you might use it wisely both for your own benefit and for the benefit of those who you love.

4 Now ask your power animal to tell you a truth about yourself that you may find difficult to hear. It might tell you that you are being lazy about getting new work in your freelance business or that you are abusing your body by eating the wrong foods, drinking too much and not getting enough rest. Take a deep breath and fully accept what your power animal has to say, knowing it has told you this out of love, respect and belief in you as a person. Ask it to help you work on these problems and ask for a sign in the next days of a good way to go about addressing them.

ANIMALS AS TEACHERS AND GUIDES

APPRECIATING YOUR ANIMAL QUALITIES

BEING ADAPTABLE

Animals are experts at adapting to reality. If they live in a cold climate, they will grow a heavy fur coat and insulating layers of fat; if they live in a hot climate, they will disperse heat through their tongues or large ears. Every moment, they have to respond to what is going on around them, in order to eat and survive. Every day we too have to adapt and shape-shift to meet the many demands made on our time, at work, at home and in our environment.

Ask your power animal to help you appreciate your own animal instinct for adapting to moment-to-moment changes throughout your day. Let it teach you how to adapt to life as it presents itself with more skill and less stress.

RHYTHM AND BALANCE

Animals have a rhythm to their lives. They hunt, feed, eliminate, rest, play, hang out with friends, care for their young, indulge in 'romance' and sex. This is not so different to us, except that we usually don't manage our lives nearly as well. We have problems honouring our basic animal needs for a good diet, adequate play and rest. We experience conflict in our version of the hunt, which is our work. We have great difficulty accepting and loving our body, validating our sexual desires and negotiating our courting rituals.

Ask your power animal to help you accept, develop and celebrate your animal needs and desires – from fully enjoying your sensuality and sexuality to successfully competing in the world to make a comfortable living. This should help you bring rhythm and balance to all aspects of your life.

REALIZE YOUR POTENTIAL

Every animal is born with a unique set of qualities and skills. The fox is a keen observer, but it is small and not strong enough to wrestle a bear. The dolphin is an excellent swimmer and communicator, but it cannot exist on land. Ask your power animal to teach you to realize your potential by accepting and developing your unique gifts.

EMBRACE THE MOMENT

Animals live fully in the moment with no fear or knowledge of their ultimate demise. Ask your power animal to help you embrace your life fully and to let each moment die so you can be born into the next. If you lose your job, ask your power animal to teach you how to shrug it off and be ready for the next opportunity. If bad weather is on the horizon, let it show you how to drink in the exhilarating perfume that pervades the air right before a storm. When it is time to leave your body, let your power animal teach you to experience it not as an end, but as a transition, perhaps to be reborn into another life.

ANIMAL ORACLES

Working with a power animal can open you to real-world animals as oracles and messengers. Our ancestors, having a special kinship with animals, saw them as messengers from the divine. For example, if a crow landed on a fence three days in a row, it might hold a special message for them. They were receptive to the signs when they appeared and were able to interpret them accurately within the context of their lives.

Through this process of receiving, deciphering and contemplating animal oracle messages, our ancestors might come to terms with the death of a loved one, understand a current difficulty in their community or be warned of future danger and misfortune. By paying close attention to their animal messengers, ancient peoples sought to expand their consciousness and transcend their limited egos and ordinary minds. In this way, they sought divine wisdom to help them through everyday life.

Almost all cultures have had a tradition of recognizing and consulting animal oracles. For example, in 300 BCE, Romulus, a Roman king, established the first college of 'augurs'. The augurs' job was to consult bird oracles to determine if the gods approved of the king's policies. In old Tibet, Buddhist lamas referred to a 9th-century Sanskrit text, 'Investigating the Cries of Crows', in order to foretell coming events. In the Americas, all indigenous tribes consulted animal oracles for 'medicine', with the aim of keeping them in a harmonious relationship with the 'Great Mystery'.

Even Shakespeare wrote of animal oracles. Lady Macbeth, while waiting for her husband to murder Duncan, is startled by an owl. She immediately recognizes that the owl is an oracle – 'the fatal bellman', or a harbinger of death.

In order to open yourself to animal oracles, try the following exercise.

PREPARING TO RECEIVE ANIMAL ORACLE GUIDANCE

1 If possible, find a quiet place in nature where you can be alone.

2 Close your eyes. Generate a sense of warm openness and receptivity to the animal world. Then bring to mind a problem you want to address.

3 Visualize an animal, a bird, an insect, a water animal or a reptile bringing you a message or a sign that will help you solve your problem. Stay with this image for as long as you can; then open your eyes and return to the present.

4 For the following few weeks, begin to attune yourself to the birds, animals and insects in your environment. Don't force an encounter, but if an animal inexplicably show ups and watches you, or if one chatters outside your window until you look up and acknowledge it, it may be an oracle. When you encounter an animal oracle, you will know because you will feel the effects in your whole body. Meditate on the animal oracle to decipher the meaning of its appearance.

ANIMALS IN DREAMS

All dream symbols contain many layers of meaning. The Power Animals Directory provides dream associations for 75 power animals to help you begin the process of analyzing your dream. When you dream of an animal, consult the Directory and then start to 'peel the onion', exploring the layered meaning of the dream animal as it relates to your own life.

FINDING MEANING

One way to discover the personal meaning of your dream is to become each aspect of the dream, both animate and inanimate and speak as best you can in its 'voice'. For example, if you dream of an outdoor scene, become the tree, become the grass, become the pond, the clouds and the animal itself.

Speak or write what each element has to 'say'. For example, you might begin with: 'I am the tree. I am huge, dark and looming over everything around me. I feel depressed.' Or you might say: 'I am the tree. I am a young sapling, fresh, innocent and a bit vulnerable.' Since each element is an aspect of you, becoming them as they appeared in the dream will give you a tremendous amount of information. In the same way, become the dream animal.

Any aspect of the dream, from a small leaf to the animal itself, can provide you with a wealth of psychological, emotional and spiritual insight about yourself at this moment in time. If your power animal appears in your dream, you can assume it is there to teach you something significant.

HOW TO RECORD YOUR DREAMS

It is best to get into the habit of recording all your dreams as soon as you wake. Use your power animal journal to record any dreams you have about animals. Dreams are ephemeral and can easily disappear from your memory.

Immediately upon waking, write down everything you can recall. Describe your entire dream. Record every detail, no matter how bizarre or trivial or disturbing it may seem. Pay particular attention to the animal that appears in your dream. Note its colour, size, demeanour and any emotions it stirred in you. Was it friendly, aggressive or simply going about its business? What did it do, if anything? If it spoke in some way, write down what it said. Everything in a dream has

meaning and will reveal itself as you work with the material and reflect and meditate upon it over time.

If you have trouble recalling your dreams, try telling yourself at bedtime that you will remember your dreams when you awake. Upon waking, move as little as possible. Reach for your journal, without fully sitting up, and begin to write. Once you sit up or get up from bed and enter full waking consciousness, your dreams will quickly fade.

SPIRIT JOURNEYS WITH YOUR POWER ANIMAL

The following four exercises will help you learn ways to imaginatively engage with your power animal. Approach them with an open mind and be receptive to whatever emerges.

You may gain insight from your power animal during the exercise or in the following days or weeks. After each exercise, record your experience in your power animal journal.

CALLING YOUR POWER ANIMAL TO YOU

Your power animal is always with you, but it helps to actually call it forward so you can consciously engage with its energy. You can do this by drumming, chanting or singing.

1 Find a time when you can be alone. Breathe deeply for a few minutes to relax and centre yourself. Then, while sitting or standing, begin drumming, chanting or singing in any way you like with the intention of calling your animal to you. If you have never done anything like this before, don't worry. Experiment and play with sound and your voice. If you are so moved, make up a short song to use on an ongoing basis.

2 Imagine that your power animal appears in front of you. Allow it to speak to you telepathically, mind to mind, about itself. Then ask your power animal what it can teach you. Ask it how it might help you in various areas of your life – in your career, in your relationships or your financial life.

3 When you feel ready, thank your power animal and ask it to stay nearby to help and guide you on a daily basis.

BECOMING YOUR POWER ANIMAL

After spending time learning everything you can about your power animal, try imaginatively becoming your power animal and take an imaginary trip to its habitat.

1 Find time to be alone and close your eyes and breathe deeply for a few minutes to enter a relaxed state.

2 Now, imagine you are your power animal and you are in its habitat. For example, if you are a female bear, imagine yourself standing upright on your hind legs in your forest home. Look down at your large, dark, fur-covered body.

Imagine you are about to dip your large paw into a beehive to extract the honey. The bees are swirling around you but you know they cannot hurt you. You enjoy the honey and turn away to walk into a grove of trees. Sniff the air, enjoying the dozens of smells with your supersensitive nose. Satisfied, begin to rub your furry back against the rough bark of a large tree.

3 Continue your visualization for as long as you are enjoying yourself. When you wish to return to your own body, thank your power animal for allowing you take on its form and visit its home. How did that feel to you? What did you learn?

IMITATING YOUR POWER ANIMAL

In indigenous cultures, the shaman would shape-shift into the form of the animal in order to understand it better and receive its messages.

1 If possible, watch a video of your animal and note carefully how it looks, moves and sounds. If you feel artistic, create a mask or animal costume ahead of time to wear during the exercise.

2 Be sure you are alone and undisturbed. If you have one, don your mask or costume. Sit or stand and breathe deeply ten times to relax and prepare to become your power animal.

3 Now, imagine you have shape-shifted into your power animal in real life. If you are a bird, imagine you have feathers, a beak, wings and bird feet. Look down and note your colouring and admire your beauty. Slowly begin to move as your power animal would move – flap your wings, turn or cock your head and caw or sing. If you are an animal, look down at your body and admire your fur, extend your claws, stamp your hooves, wiggle your snout and bare your teeth. If you are a water animal, feel yourself moving effortlessly through your lake, river or ocean. Actually move around the room as your animal would.

4 As you enter your animal's reality, note how you feel. Do you feel fearful, powerful, more beautiful, more confident? Do you feel more or less like yourself, do you feel comfortable imagining you are your power animal?

5 When you are ready, sit or stand quietly and 're-enter' your own body. Thank your power animal for letting you experience its reality and for any insights you may have gained.

UNCOVERING THE SOURCE OF DIFFICULTY

Choose a recent problem or event that you have had difficulty understanding or resolving. In this exercise, you will engage your power animal's help in finding the source of your problem.

1 Sit on a chair or stretch out on the floor, keeping your spine straight. Close your eyes and breathe deeply for a few minutes to relax and ready yourself for your journey.

2 Imagine your power animal is in front of you. Ask it to guide you back in time to the source of the current problem that you are experiencing. For example, if you are having problems in your romantic relationship, your power animal may take you back to when you met this person. You may be reminded that you had misgivings when you entered the relationship. You may realize your current troubles stem partly from your own dishonesty with yourself and your ongoing fear of being alone.

3 Return with your power animal to the present. Whether you feel you have learned anything about the source of your problem or not, thank your power animal for its time, effort and support.

ANIMAL PROTECTORS

ANIMALS AS GUARDIANS AND SPIRIT COMPANIONS

We all want and need protection from harm. One of the main functions of your power animal is to protect and defend you from danger of all kinds. This is why Native American warriors painted their power animal's image on their shields. If you feel vulnerable or afraid in any way, your power animal can help you feel stronger and safer, by protecting you and teaching you how to protect yourself better.

As described in the Directory, your power animal excels at specific ways of protecting, and knowing its 'speciality' can help you gain the most from your relationship. For example, the lizard protects from psychological manipulation and the mouse protects you when signing contracts. However, that said, all power animals are fully capable of protecting and defending you from all forms of danger.

PROTECTING DURING TRAVEL

This simple exercise helps you feel and be safer when travelling or when using public transportation.

1 Before you leave your home, invite your power animal to accompany you and ask for its protection against accident, theft or bodily harm.

2 Imagine your power animal walking, flying or swimming alongside you. Feel its power and protective energy. Know that it will remain awake at your side even while you sleep. Ask it to provide a second pair of eyes to help you protect your valuables and belongings. Ask it to alert you to any potential accident or physical harm.

3 When you return home, take the time to thank your power animal for its companionship and protection.

PROTECTING FROM VERBAL ABUSE

This exercise helps you simultaneously heal from childhood and adult wounding and teaches you how to protect yourself in the future by engaging the help of your power animal.

1 Recall a difficult encounter from your past with a friend, relative or co-worker or any other person. Perhaps he or she attacked you with barbed jokes or verbally abused you. The person also may have said nothing, but directed his or her venom and negativity at you. Feel the pain you felt at that time, then let it go.

2 Now relive the scene, only this time imagine your power animal standing at your left shoulder. Feel the strength and power of its presence. If it is small, imagine it human-sized. If it is large, let it remain its normal size. Imagine your power animal's aura extending for a fair distance, surrounding both of you and forming a shield against the negative words and thoughts coming your way. Know that nothing this person says or thinks can really harm you.

3 When you find yourself in a similar situation, immediately summon your power animal to your side. Feel its protective aura surrounding both of you. If you choose to, respond and defend yourself, but refrain from attacking in return. If the person does not stop attacking, end the conversation. If you want to maintain this relationship, set boundaries and conditions under which you are willing to talk in the future and leave with your power animal.

PROTECTING YOUR LIFE ENERGY

One way to guard and protect yourself is to preserve and protect your chi or your life force. Your power animal helps you protect and maintain your energy, which leaves you less vulnerable to harm.

1 For 24 hours, imagine your power animal at your side, at home, at work and any other place you might be. Ask your power animal to help you notice when you are pushing yourself, stressing out, running too fast, not eating well, not getting enough exercise or sleep. Ask it to point out symptoms such as confusion, fatigue, nausea, light-headedness or 'spaciness'.

2 Ask your power animal to suggest ways in which you can preserve and maintain your energy, thus leaving you less vulnerable to attack, manipulation or loss. Write down what advice your power animal communicates in your journal.

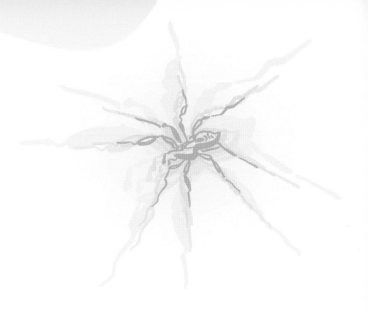

PROTECTING YOUR ENERGY FIELD

When you protect your aura or your energy field, you protect your boundaries from being breached by negative thoughts, feelings and projections sent to you by others. When you allow your boundaries to be breached, you will feel depleted, depressed and drained of energy. A healthy boundary is flexible and allows in good support, but keeps out whatever is toxic. You can learn to adjust its rigidity or permeability to protect yourself better from harm.

The mere presence of certain situations and people can also drain your energy and leave you feeling negative, powerless or irritated. Certain television programmes, movies, the internet and reading material can also deplete your energy and leave you feeling violated.

1 For one week, ask your power animal to help you identify when you feel assaulted by negative energy, situations or people. For example, if you have an interaction with a certain co-worker in the morning, you may notice you feel 'off' for the rest of the day. Write down any instances in your journal, and note the effect they have on your energy. Also list your own activities that leave you feeling less positive and protected. Perhaps you are taking in too many crime shows and violent images into your consciousness, that are damaging your aural field and making you feel weak and vulnerable.

2 Ask your power animal to help you identify creative ways to protect yourself from external negative forces and your own internal negative habits. For example, it may suggest that when your co-worker is sending you negative vibes, you visualize your aura as an impermeable protective shield. Or it may ask you to monitor and eliminate media that are weakening you, causing you to feel afraid and vulnerable.

ANIMALS AS MAGICAL FAMILIARS

A familiar is another word for power animal. The definition of 'familiar' is a companion animal which attends or serves a person. In world folklore, familiars are often associated with witches and have a somewhat negative connotation. However, not all witches are evil. In fairytales and real life they often use their magic for good, by casting spells for love, health and wealth. Modern-day witches – practitioners of witchcraft and other pagan traditions – believe in using their powers only for beneficial purposes.

The witch, or wise woman, often had an animal or 'familiar' that served as her companion and helper. Folk tales describe familiars as cats, snakes, owls, squirrels, dogs, birds or toads. These, however, were not ordinary animals. The witch had a deep connection and attunement with her familiar and it functioned as her partner in her work. Highly sensitive to psychic vibrations, her familiar would alert her to negative energy in an individual or her environment. She and her familiar had the ability to communicate telepathically. Her familiar, as her protector, also had the role of shielding her from psychic and physical harm.

At times her familiar would be a magical animal because it was more flexible and could assist her better in her work. For example, a magical cat would be able to travel and bring back messages where real animals could not. The witch would sometimes be portrayed as riding a magical animal, which is a symbol for astral travel and the ability to access other dimensions.

The magical familiar could be thought of as the witch's power animal. In fact, it may be helpful to think of your power animal as your magical familiar. Your power animal is not just an imaginary pet. It provides you with a link to the animal kingdom and the essence of their power, but also possesses magical qualities in itself. Your power animal is your familiar. It is there to serve you, protect you and attend you as you go about your everyday life. It is highly attuned to you and your needs.

BONDING WITH YOUR POWER ANIMAL AS YOUR MAGICAL FAMILIAR

This simple exercise will help you deepen your understanding of your power animal and recognize it as your familiar.

1 Close your eyes and breathe deeply for a few minutes to feel relaxed and centred. Imagine your power animal very close in front of you. Reach out and touch it, stroking it gently and lovingly. Match your breathing with its breathing.

Look into its eyes and see that it is much more than an ordinary animal. It is indeed magical, possesses extraordinary intelligence and has intimate knowledge of who you are.

2 Tell your power animal that you recognize and accept its devotion, protection and service to you. Thank it for the gifts and help it has already shared.

ANIMAL AMULETS

The use of amulets is found across all human cultures and eras, and stems from the universal desire to be protected from harm. The word 'amulet' is derived from the Latin word *amuletum*, meaning 'means of defence'. The Arabic word for amulet is *hamalet*, meaning 'that which is suspended'. An amulet, then, is any object – a stone, a plant, an artefact or a piece of writing – that is suspended from the neck or tied to any part of the body and used for protection. Most amulets found in archaeological digs are often just small fragments of semi-precious stones, but some are carved into the shape of an animal or an insect.

PROTECTIVE QUALITIES

It was thought that amulets could guard against poisoning, help cure or prevent disease, aid in childbirth and protect from danger of all kinds. In particular, amulets were thought to ward off the 'evil eye', the universal belief that a person can cause harm simply by looking at someone. In virtually every language there is a term for the 'evil eye'. In German, it is the *böser blick*; in French it is *mauvais veil*; and in Italian it is *malocchio*. A famous Italian amulet for warding off the evil eye is the *cornicello*, a long, twisted, animal horn, usually carved of red coral, but also found in red plastic, silver, gold or blown glass.

The Egyptians used frog amulets to promote fertility and the scarab beetle to protect against evil spells and ensure a good afterlife. Assyrian and Babylonian men wore ram and bull amulets for strength and virility. In Africa, tribal people wore animal amulets as charm bags containing animal fur, claws or bones. People in the Middle Ages used amulets to ward off epidemics thought to be caused by evil spirits, and they wore amulet bags containing dried frogs to prevent epileptic seizure. Today, many alternative spiritual traditions make use of animal amulets for protection, as do those people who work with power animals or totems. Wearing or carrying an amulet of your power animal will help you feel protected in any situation. For example, if you feel afraid walking alone into an enclosed car park, touching your amulet will summon your power animal for protection.

CREATE YOUR OWN ANIMAL AMULET

1 Buy a very small image of your power animal made of stone, wood or metal, or create one of your own by carving it in wood, modelling it in clay or incising its image on a smooth semi-precious stone such as turquoise or amber. Your amulet should be small, perhaps no larger than 2.5 cm (1 in) square.

2 Call on your personal power animal and ask it to lend its spirit to your amulet.

3 Purchase or sew a small silk bag to use for carrying your amulet or talisman. Wear it suspended from your neck, or carry it in your pocket.

ANIMAL HEALERS

ANIMAL ALTARS

Although the practice of creating home altars today is rare, we may be unconsciously creating altars in the way we group objects in our homes – for example, a grouping of our relatives' photos on the mantle or a collection of glass animal figures displayed in a glass cabinet. But the spiritual benefits are lost because these 'altars' are not created with sacred intention or purpose. Consciously making an altar will help you create sacred space and deepen your relationship with your power animal.

An altar is a wonderful tool for focusing your concentration and connecting to the spiritual realms within yourself. When working with your power animal for healing, an altar will help speed your progress because it encourages daily meditation and communication. In many ways, the power of the altar lies in its visibility. The objects on your altar give form to the imaginative relationship you have with your power animal. They physically symbolize your animal's invisible qualities and gifts and help you manifest them in your own life. The simple act of lighting a candle or incense will also help you connect you with the power of ritual to transform your life.

CREATING YOUR POWER ANIMAL ALTAR

Your altar can be as complex or simple as you like. If you are short on space, use a small shelf, a screened-in porch, a walk-in closet or any other quiet nook where you can be alone.

1 Begin by creating a sacred space. Clean it thoroughly and mentally dedicate it to your power animal and your own growth and development.

2 Begin by placing a small table or chest of drawers or shelf in the space you have created to serve as the base of your altar. Cover it with a beautiful cloth or scarf. On it, artfully arrange as many images as you want of your power animal or animals, if you have more than one. Include drawings, photos or statues. If possible, use special frames for the photos and small stands for the statues.

3 Add symbols of the natural world, such as a crystal or a beautiful stone and, if possible, twigs, leaves or other items from your animal's environment. Make sure the objects you choose inspire you, centre you and stimulate your creativity and imagination. Each item should be meaningful to you rather than just decorative. Their purpose is to help you make a strong connection with your power animal.

4 Place a candle, a small bowl of water, a small amount of earth and incense on your altar to represent the four elements.

5 Place a cushion or chair in front of or nearby your altar, ready to use when you want to meditate on your power animal. Keep your power animal journal on your altar when not in use.

ANIMAL SPIRIT MEDICINE

The term 'medicine' in the Native American tradition means anything that helps you to connect to the sacredness of all reality. Animal spirit medicine is rooted in nature and the animal world. It includes the healing of your body, mind and spirit, the development of personal power and the maintenance of harmony and balance with the universe. Animal spirit medicine is similar to the holistic approach of Buddhism and Taoism in that it is an all-encompassing way of life.

HEALING OF BODY MIND AND SPIRIT

Animal spirit medicine refers to the power or 'medicine' that your power animal offers you. For example, if your power animal is the squirrel, it has the power to store energy and ideas. It is a great planner and will help you let go of things you no longer need. It can also help you manage your physical energy. Yet, before you can make use of its medicine, you may need to first heal your past.

After you identify your power animal, you may find you need emotional, physical or spiritual healing in relation to its particular skills. If so, in the past you may have failed to develop your totem's qualities or, not having them, you got into trouble in some way. Using the squirrel example above, perhaps in the past your failure to plan caused you to lose your life savings or destroyed your car's engine. Or, because you lost your spiritual moorings, you ran up a huge credit card bill, hoping, in some desperate way, to find spiritual fulfilment at the shopping mall. In other words, before you access squirrel's medicine, you may need to heal from not having it.

The cells of your body hold the memory of your past and present emotional traumas. Any aspect of emotional energy that has not been healed affects the health of your entire being. Your power animal helps you heal any past physical, emotional or spiritual traumas, by reconnecting you with nature and the sacred.

HEALING FROM LACK OF MEDICINE

This exercise will help you let go of any past trauma connected with your power animal's medicine. Gather your power animal journal and find time to be alone.

1 Describe your power animal's medicine and how not having or using its qualities and gifts may have caused you to suffer in the past. Describe in detail two or three events or situations where you were deeply embarrassed, suffered loss or failed in some way that was painful to you.

2 Ask your power animal to help you release any residual shame or pain caused by not having its skills or qualities. Tell it you are willing to learn to use its medicine, to avoid self-sabotage and harm to others and become a positive force in the world. Ask your power animal to show you how to renew your connection with nature and begin to feel and experience the world as sacred.

3 Write down any messages or answers that come to you, either now or in the weeks ahead.

DEVELOPMENT OF PERSONAL POWER

Power is a confusing word that can have many meanings. In the power animal world, spirit medicine is never expressed as power over anyone else. The positive expression of power is the manifestation of your unique qualities and gifts, for the benefit of yourself and others. Animal spirit medicine is concerned with consequences of the use of power. In the Native American tradition, the effect of your actions on others must be considered for seven generations ahead.

Your power animal will also help you come to terms with the qualities you have and don't have. For example, you may want to have a buffalo for your power animal because you would like to make the biggest mark possible on the world. You may want buffalo's great size and presence to help you stand out and appear more powerful than everyone else in the room. This may reflect your denial of your own real nature and gifts, as well as a grave misunderstanding and use of buffalo's medicine.

As you develop your relationship with your power animal, you will come to a greater appreciation of your own medicine and how to use it responsibly in the world. As you give up fantasies of the person you would like to be, you will embrace who you really are. Your totem animal will help you manifest your own authentic power. As you heal from your past, you will find a place in the world that is uniquely yours.

MAINTAINING HARMONY AND BALANCE WITH THE UNIVERSE

Unfortunately, many of us live much of our life indoors without any natural light. Our fast-paced world keeps us in a state of perpetual reactivity. Our time seems to be owned by others – our boss, our spouse, the relatives, the kids or our friends. It is very easy, in the world we live in today, to lose sight of our internal compass. And what is left of our internal compass has long since detached from the natural rhythms and cycles of the Earth.

Working with and meditating on your power animal will gradually reintroduce you to nature. You will begin to honour your body and its needs and make time for relaxation and reflection. You may begin to balance the competing areas of your life, making small adjustments, increasing the time you spend doing the things you really love. Over time, your affection for animals and nature will grow and eventually you will have a full-blown love affair with Mother Earth. You will feel the desire and necessity to harmonize your life with hers.

ANIMAL HEALING MEDITATIONS

The following healing meditations are to be used in conjunction with treatment from your doctor or other medical practitioner. They are meant to enhance and augment traditional modalities and to help speed healing and recovery. They are not, however, a substitute for professional health care which should always be carried out through a qualified doctor. With that caveat in mind, working with your power animal as a healer is one of the most powerful ways to improve your life. Even if you have not been diagnosed with an illness, meditating on your power animal can help you prevent imbalances that lead to disease and help you maintain your health resolutions.

MAINTAINING YOUR PHYSICAL HEALTH

Many of us want to lose weight, eat better, exercise and get sufficient sleep, but (as the saying goes) 'the road to hell is paved with good intentions'. Enlisting your power animal's support can help you stay on track.

1 Find time when you can be alone and undisturbed. Lie down, close your eyes and make yourself comfortable. Beginning with your toes and working up to your crown, scan your body for any tension. Breathe deeply and fully relax.

2 Imagine you are visiting your power animal in its habitat. You have met it in a clearing and have taken a seat directly in front of it. Notice how your power animal appears healthy, radiant and full of vitality.

3 Ask your power animal to communicate to you, telepathically, what you should do to maintain your physical health. If you don't understand something it says to you, press for clarity. Are there any surprises?

4 Ask your power animal to help you on a daily basis to be consistent in acting on its suggestions.

5 End your meditation and record what your power animal had to say in your power animal journal.

HEALING FROM ILLNESS

If you have a chronic or serious illness, the following meditation will help to boost your immune system.

1 Find time when you can be alone and undisturbed. Lie down and make yourself comfortable. Close your eyes. Beginning with your toes and working up to your crown, scan your body for any tension. Breathe deeply and fully relax.

2 Bring to mind the condition or illness you would like to heal. Feel any emotions you may have. If you feel fear or anger or sadness, let those feelings emerge, feel them and then see them moving on from you like clouds moving across the sky. Take as long as you need.

3 When you are ready, mentally invite your power animal to sit quietly at your right side. It does not matter if it is large or small. It can be an elephant or a bee. You are in an imaginative world and all things are possible. Feel your power animal's presence as benevolent and caring. Mentally reach out and touch your power animal. Feel its fur or feathers or skin. Now imagine your power animal's energy transferring through your hand into your body, filling you from head to toe with healing gold light. Imagine this gold light washing away whatever is causing your illness. For example, if you have arthritis, see the inflammation in your joints clearing. If you have diabetes, see your blood sugar as stable and healthy. If you have cancer, see the cancer cells shrivelling in the powerful golden light streaming from your animal.

4 Stay with this visualization as long as you like, and then remove your hand from your power animal. Thank it for agreeing to lend its energy to help you heal.

EMOTIONAL HEALING

We all, at one time or another, suffer emotional trauma. It could be from the death of a loved one, the end of a relationship, financial problems or simply the accumulation of unrelieved emotional stress over time. Your power animal can help you overcome the trauma with emotional healing.

1 Find a time when you can be alone, outdoors and undisturbed. Find a place where you can sit, perhaps on a chair in your garden or a tree stump in the forest. Choose a spot that appeals and where you are physically comfortable.

2 Close your eyes and breathe deeply for a few minutes to relax and clear your mind of extraneous thoughts. Begin to smell the air around you and listen to the sounds of birds, insects, the wind in the trees and flowing water if it is nearby.

3 Now, with your eyes still closed, imagine your power animal appears about 1.5 m (5 ft) in front of you. For example, if it is a horse, see it standing slightly turned to the side, its beautiful eyes looking intently at you. If it is a dragonfly,

see it perched on a small rock, its iridescence gleaming in the sun.

4 Mentally begin to talk to your power animal, telling it what is bothering you. Don't worry if you don't have a clear idea of why you are troubled, simply begin to say everything on your mind. Your power animal will wait patiently for as long as you need to vent.

5 Now mentally trade places with your power animal. Become your power animal and see yourself seated in front of you. Take a moment to fully feel yourself in your power animal's body. As your power animal, feel compassion for the person in front of you (yourself). As your power animal, telepathically communicate to yourself what you see as the source of your problems and the best way to heal yourself emotionally.

6 When your power animal finishes what it has to say to you, switch places and become yourself again. Thank your power animal for its wisdom and compassion.

REAL ANIMALS AS HEALERS

In 1980, an American study of heart-attack victims accidentally discovered that patients with pets recovered faster and lived longer than those without. An Australian study, conducted in 1992, concluded that pet owners had significantly lower blood pressure, triglyceride and cholesterol levels than people who did not own pets. Today, in upstate New York, troubled inner-city kids attend a special school where caring for farm animals is a central part of their therapy, education and rehabilitation. Caring for animals provides them with a gateway for relating better with people. In New York City, in September 2001, therapy dogs comforted the rescue workers after the attacks on the World Trade Center. Many grown men wept into the dogs' fur.

HOW ANIMALS HELP HUMANS

The list of animal-related health studies gets longer each year. A few more are listed below. Can there be any doubt, from this brief list, that interaction with animals is profoundly healing?

- One study showed that minor health complaints decrease after adopting a pet.
- Another study revealed that women have lower stress levels in the presence of their dogs as compared to a best friend.
- Children who care for pets score higher in measures of empathy and self-esteem.
- Mentally challenged children show significant progress after interacting with dolphins and sea turtles.
- Having a dog in a psychotherapy session with a child accelerates therapy by providing a bridge for communication.
- Watching tropical fish swim in a tank lowers blood pressure in adults.
- The growing field of therapeutic horseriding benefits both children and adults with physical, psychological and mental disabilities.

RELIEVING STRESS

It is becoming clear that pets can provide you with some of the best and most economical complementary medicine available today. Most importantly, they can be great stress relievers within families and provide support, consistency and stability for kids growing up in a fast paced modern world. Taking your dog for a walk and observing it sniff the air, petting your cat and listening to it purr as you fall asleep, are soothing and healing activities. Simply placing your hand on your dog's fur can lower your heart rate and blood pressure and give you moral support when having a difficult conversation. Caring for an animal can increase your compassion for yourself, your friends, your family and your colleagues.

REACH OUT TO THE ANIMAL WORLD

This brings us back to where we started – with the animal drawings of our ancestors in the caves in France and the animal totem poles of Native Americans. Clearly, our ancestors deeply valued and honoured their animal brothers and sisters. Unfortunately, in our march to modernity, we devalued the sacredness of the human–animal relationship. Using sophisticated scientific studies, we are rediscovering what our ancestors knew long ago: our relationship with the animal world is not only good for us, it may even be necessary for our health and wellbeing.

POWER ANIMALS
DIRECTORY

INTERPRETATION GUIDE

As a dream symbol
Soul, introspection, inner vision,
strength, transformation

As a guardian or protector
Protects children
Develops strong boundaries

As a healer
Promotes balance and harmony
Recommends herbal remedies

As an oracle or omen
Rely on your inner wisdom
Stand tall

BEAR

MYTHS AND STORIES

This largest of carnivores is associated with
the goddesses Artemis and Diana and the
lunar cycle. Ancient Nordic warriors, called
the 'Berserkers', wore bear shirts into battle,
hoping to embody the bear's immense
fighting abilities.

IF BEAR IS YOUR POWER ANIMAL

You have an imposing presence and strong
confidence in your abilities. When those you
love are threatened, especially children, you
defend them ferociously. Your sense of smell is
unusually keen. You are a connoisseur of the
sweet things in life – a gourmet dessert, a love
affair, a fragrant flower. Creative projects that
require sustained effort over two or more
years are your strong suit. Those around you
put up with your occasional moods because of
your strength and grounded personality.

ASK BEAR TO HELP YOU

- Live a more balanced and harmonious life
- Use introspection and meditation to
  achieve your goals
- Discover your untapped, inner resources
- Be more self-reliant

ACCESS BEAR'S POWER BY

- Going on a spiritual retreat during the
  winter months
- Visiting a beekeeper and learning about the
  activity of bees

*Bears are associated with crystals found deep in
the caves where they hibernate. Crystals heal
through resonance and vibration and the
realignment of subtle energies. If bear is your
power animal, explore using quartz crystals for
healing your body, mind and spirit.*

INTERPRETATION GUIDE

As a dream symbol
Innocence, femininity, gentleness,
seduction, love, compassion, altruism

As a guardian or protector
Protects through invisibility
Guards newborn babies

As a healer
Recommends peaceful environments
Encourages physical renewal

As an oracle or omen
Trust your instincts
Let go of anger and hostility

DEER

MYTHS AND STORIES

The Buddha gave his first teaching in the Deer Park at Sarnath, India. Many ancient cultures identified the deer with rebirth, because it sheds and regrows its antlers. The ancient Japanese considered deer to be intermediaries between humans and gods.

IF DEER IS YOUR POWER ANIMAL

You are extremely sensitive. You observe very subtle changes in people and your surroundings that others miss. In relationships, you hear what is not said. Nature and the countryside appeal to you more than the excitement of urban life. When faced with a challenge, you rely on your instincts and quickly decide what action is appropriate. At times you use seduction and appearance to achieve your goals. In your best moments, you rely on love and compassion.

ASK DEER TO HELP YOU

- Be graceful and gentle in your manner and movement
- Validate your sensitive nature and the need for sensitivity in human relationships
- Apply the power of love to solve problems at home, work and in your community

ACCESS DEER'S POWER BY

- Practising deep listening when in conversation with friends and family
- Decorating your home in restful natural and neutral colours

Deer tend to feed at dawn and dusk at the edges of forests, when they blend in best with their surroundings. They can see extremely well in low light. When a situation is murky and complicated, call on the deer to help you 'see' the truth.

As a dream symbol
Threat, truth, loyalty, social status,
kinship, joy

As a guardian or protector
Guards you from acting inappropriately
Helps you define boundaries

As a healer
Helps heal family relationships
Restores strength after illness

As an oracle or omen
Freedom requires discipline
Face your problems

WOLF

MYTHS AND STORIES

Romulus and Remus, the twin founders of
Rome, were suckled by a she-wolf. The
phrase 'A wolf in sheep's clothing' comes
from the Aesop tale in which a wolf dresses
as a sheep to attack the rest of the flock. The
wolf is discovered, but gets entangled in his
disguise and is killed.

IF WOLF IS YOUR POWER ANIMAL

You love family and community and feel lost
without them. Rules, rituals and social
hierarchies provide you with a feeling of
safety and comfort. Most people find you
warm and affectionate. The language of the
heart interests you most. You are highly
intelligent and a natural teacher. You help
others discover their path in life. When
negative, you accurately assess and take
advantage of other's weaknesses.

ASK WOLF TO HELP YOU

- Examine your various masks and personas
  – seductress, victim, executive, innocent –
  and let them go one by one
- Find the balance between being socially
  isolated or too enmeshed in relationships
- Be less ruthless in your business affairs

ACCESS WOLF'S POWER BY

- Getting involved in local politics
- Organizing a family reunion
- Teaching a course in a subject that
  interests you

Wolves live in family groups called packs. Animal
*behaviourists believe the members of a pack have a
strong affection for one another. Celebrate your
family relationships by cooking a special meal to
show your loved ones how much you care for them.*

As a dream symbol
Trickster, fool, chaos, risk, self-sabotage, hidden wisdom, humour

As a guardian or protector
Guards against life's pitfalls
Protects from inflated sense of self

As a healer
Heals with laughter
Relieves depression

As an oracle or omen
Expect a hard lesson
Have more fun in your life

COYOTE

MYTHS AND STORIES

The *Heyoka*, jesters of the Lakota tribe who teach wisdom through satire, consider coyote their mentor. The Navahos credit this mischievous trickster with creating humans and the Milky Way.

IF COYOTE IS YOUR POWER ANIMAL

You are a practical joker and a consummate survivor. You take risks that frighten most mortals. You are highly intelligent and creative, yet will play the fool or buffoon to get what you want. Because you cannot see the obvious, you comically and tragically make the same mistakes over and over again. You are able to find wisdom and humour in any situation, however disastrous.

ASK COYOTE TO HELP YOU

- Take yourself less seriously
- Examine your hidden desires
- Notice how you play the trickster with others by holding back information or pretending to be what you are not

ACCESS COYOTE'S POWER BY

- Remembering a time when you allowed yourself to be taken in by someone, or you tried to deceive someone else
- Using humour to attract your mate or teach your children an important lesson

---

Native Americans regard the coyote as a clever trickster, an enthusiastic fool and a consummate survivor. If coyote is your power animal, also examine the Fool card from the Tarot. Have the courage to take risks and be rewarded with a full and wonderful life.

As a dream symbol
Beauty, craftiness, disguise, stamina,
intelligence, supernatural power

As a guardian or protector
Makes a good parent
Protects the family unit

As a healer
Helps integrate thought and emotion
Harmonizes relationships

As an oracle or omen
Watch for deception
Pay attention to body language

FOX

MYTHS AND STORIES

Both Native American and Chinese lore tell
of the fox transforming into a beautiful
woman. In a famous European folk tale,
'Reynaud the Fox' preyed on nobility and
peasants alike, but went unpunished because
of his cleverness.

IF FOX IS YOUR POWER ANIMAL

You are a night person and your best
creative work is done while others sleep.
Your instinct is to be monogamous and mate
for life, but you also require long periods of
solitude. You are highly intelligent, a keen
observer of people and situations and a
great judge of character. You can blend into
your surroundings and are expert at
concealment and disguises. At times, you
charm or clown in order to camouflage your
real intentions.

ASK FOX TO HELP YOU

- Transform your ability to deceive and trick
  into creative energy that can be used to
  benefit others
- Use your cleverness and charm to make
  your workplace a better place for
  everyone
- Employ your observation skills in improving
  your family and work relationships

ACCESS FOX'S POWER BY

- Imagining you are invisible at a party and
  then carefully observing the other guests
- Learning magic tricks

In the spring and summer, the Arctic fox has a
dark coat; in the autumn and winter, it turns white,
to blend in with the snow. Try changing your own
hair colour to express your feelings at different
times of the year.

As a dream symbol
Courage, aggression, endurance, perseverance, healing, truth

As a guardian or protector
Protects your back
Teaches self-defence

As a healer
Promotes deep systemic healing
Clears energy blockages

As an oracle or omen
Fight for what you want
Persevere in completing projects

BADGER

MYTHS AND STORIES

For Native Americans, the badger is the power animal of medicine women, the keeper of medicinal roots. In European folklore the badger represents endurance and courage under attack.

IF BADGER IS YOUR POWER ANIMAL

You have a great interest in alternative medicine, especially mineral, root and herb remedies. The rough exterior face you show the world is intimidating to most. Your aggressive nature and your ability to work hard and complete projects puts you on top of your chosen field. It is impossible to keep secrets around you, as you will dig down beneath the surface to find answers. You freely express your emotions and have strong mental energy. In a crisis, you stay grounded and focused, and do not panic.

ASK BADGER TO HELP YOU

- Overcome any fear around your job
- Learn how to focus, work hard and persist in achieving your goals
- Express yourself boldly and honestly, without fear of consequences
- Build or repair the basement or foundation of your house

ACCESS BADGER'S POWER BY

- Visiting 'underground' architecture, one with three walls nestled into the side of a hill
- Visiting your local health food store and exploring natural remedies

Native Americans called those who loved the warmth of fire 'Badger people'. The badger is also known as a great storyteller, a keeper of history, legend and lore. Recall the stories you loved as a child, especially those told around a camp fire.

HORSE

MYTHS AND STORIES

In Greek myth, Pegasus, the winged horse, was born from the blood of the snake-haired goddess Medusa. The centaur Chiron, half man and half horse, was rejected at birth by his human mother. He healed his wounds and having done so, became a great compassionate healer. In Celtic myth, white horses are associated with the goddesses Rhiannon and Epona.

IF HORSE IS YOUR POWER ANIMAL

You are highly sensitive and react strongly to your surroundings. You value harmonious social relationships and if not called upon to lead, you are happy to follow. When members of your extended family are not getting along, they turn to you for mediation. Your biggest personal fear is being rejected. You have great endurance and enjoy your freedom to travel. You may have difficulty in learning to trust, but when you do, you give your heart fully.

ASK HORSE TO HELP YOU

- Realize your desire for travel and adventure
- Be a compassionate and effective leader in your community

ACCESS HORSE'S POWER BY

- Visiting a stable and riding a horse
- Running in a marathon

There are over 150 breeds of horses and ponies. Is your power horse a thoroughbred, draught horse, stallion, gelding or mare? What colour is it? Imagine that you are your horse. How does it feel to be so beautiful, powerful and free?

As a dream symbol
Mother, nourishment, abundance,
sacrifice, gentleness, humility

As a guardian or protector
Protects family relations
Guards against loss of home

As a healer
Heals digestion
Promotes relaxation

As an oracle or omen
You need nourishment
Learn to cooperate

COW

MYTHS AND STORIES

Nut, the Egyptian goddess of the night sky, was often represented as a cow. In many cultures the cow represents the Great Mother, earth, love and abundance.

IF COW IS YOUR POWER ANIMAL

You are warm, nurturing, earthly, sensual and slow-moving – except when you are angry! The material comforts are important to you. Your home is inviting and good food always graces your table. You are deeply concerned about family relations, world peace and the environment. Having a successful marriage is important to you and you work hard at being a good spouse. You are a very thoughtful individual. You ruminate, analyze and digest before you incorporate anyone or anything into your life. Others depend on your maternal love and deep wisdom.

ASK COW TO HELP YOU

- Imagine the future of your newborn
- Move in balance with the feminine quality of nature
- Learn humility, flexibility and gentleness

ACCESS COW'S POWER BY

- Writing down a list of what you consider to be 'the good things of life'
- Taking your time to thoroughly investigate before making a decision
- Being the peacemaker in your family

Cows have a stomach with four compartments. This enables them to bring swallowed food back into their mouth to be chewed and swallowed again until fully digested. Do you chew your food thoroughly so as to release all its nutrients?

As a dream symbol
Reproduction, power, anger, strength,
speed, obstinacy, sacrifice

As a guardian or protector
Protects what is sacred
Guards against intrusion

As a healer
Provides psychological integration
Cures infertility

As an oracle or omen
Face your dark side
Don't give into rage

BULL

MYTHS AND STORIES

The Paleolithic goddess, the Venus of Laussel,
is shown holding a crescent-shaped bullhorn.
The Egyptian god Osiris was often depicted
with the head of a bull.

IF BULL IS YOUR POWER ANIMAL

You are sensitive to weather changes and can
predict the approach of storms. When
angered, you 'bellow' your displeasure and
put on an impressive display, but rarely
attack. If you do, pity your opponent. You
make the mundane and ordinary alive and
fertile. In your company, life becomes a richer
and deeper experience. You are not afraid to
mine the darker side of yourself for the gold
of personal integration, psychological insight
and spiritual wisdom.

ASK BULL TO HELP YOU

- Confront your darkest secret
- Enrich your life by finding joy
  every moment
- Manage your anger

ACCESS BULL'S POWER BY

- Studying the ancient Greek story of the
  Labyrinth and the Minotaur, a creature
  with a man's body and a bull's head
- Exploring psychotherapy as a way to
  understand your deeper nature
- Using a barometer to predict storms

Men and women of Ancient Crete practised 'bull
leaping', or jumping over a charging bull – a
precursor to modern-day Spanish bullfighting and the
annual 'running of the bulls' in Pamplona, Spain.
Practise 'taking the bull by the horns' in your own life.

INTERPRETATION GUIDE

As a dream symbol
Gratitude, health,
independence, prayer

As a guardian or protector
Protects you from becoming
unbalanced
Guards your new ventures

As a healer
Relieves spiritual alienation
Heals addiction

As an oracle or omen
Remember your connection to
everything and everyone
All your needs will be met

BUFFALO

MYTHS AND STORIES

White Buffalo Calf Woman introduced Native American people to the use of the sacred pipe. The pipe forms a bridge connecting the Earth and the Heavens and the stem and the bowl symbolize the circle of love that binds men and women.

IF BUFFALO IS YOUR POWER ANIMAL

You may feel large and powerful. When you want to, you can move very quickly. You value generosity and responsibility for others and you are also a good provider. Stubbornness is one of your problems and you often miss what is right before your eyes. Though you have great stores of energy and ability, you need to find ways to access them and to use them properly.

ASK BUFFALO TO HELP YOU

• Shoulder your responsibilities so you can make use of the gifts and abundance you have been given

• Renew your relationship with prayer

• Teach you how to be compassionate to all living beings and respectful of their individual journeys

ACCESS BUFFALO'S POWER BY

• Meditating on paintings or photographs of large buffalo herds

• Writing about how abundance manifests in your life

Native American people made practical use of every part of the buffalo they hunted. Take a moment to think about the practical ways in which other people benefit from your hands, feet, eyes, ears, mind and other parts of you.

As a dream symbol
Corruption, foundation, sexual energy,
humour, flexibility, hard work

As a guardian or protector
Guards in unchartered territories
Ensures basic needs are met

As a healer
Cures panic attacks
Heals sexual dysfunction

As an oracle or omen
Stop butting your head against the wall
Let go of guilt

GOAT

A MYTHS AND STORIES

In Egypt the goat was a symbol of nobility.
The horned goat god 'Pan' was one of the
oldest Greek deities associated with nature
and sexual energy.

IF GOAT IS YOUR POWER ANIMAL

You have great powers of endurance. You are
practical and very disciplined. When in a
good mood, you have a great sense of
humour, but when not, you can be
cantankerous, pessimistic and fatalistic. When
it comes to business deals, you are ambitious,
sure-footed and demonstrate agility in tough
situations. You often 'scale the heights' and
achieve worldly success, but always remain
down to earth. You love the material things
of life and especially sexual pleasure. Your
mischievous nature sometimes lands you in
ethical dilemmas.

ASK GOAT TO HELP YOU

• Assess the present situation accurately,
  so as to predict the future outcome
• Stay grounded and sure-footed if you
  are moving to a new home or starting
  a new job
• Be more flexible and agile when
  negotiating the day-to-day realities of
  work and family life

ACCESS GOAT'S POWER BY

• Hiking a mountain trail
• Becoming more comfortable with
  your sexuality

*Study the tenth sign of the Western zodiac,
Capricorn, which is symbolized by the goat and its
ruler the planet Saturn, known for its stern
influence. Are you sometimes too stern? If so, try
not to be so hard on yourself and others.*

As a dream symbol
Patience, renewal, purification, peace, humility, compassion, sacrifice

As a guardian or protector
Protects against violence
Guards your social group

As a healer
Purifies body
Helps heal from abuse

As an oracle or omen
Stop being indecisive
Don't follow blindly

SHEEP

MYTHS AND STORIES

The ewe was associated with the Celtic goddess Brigit and her spring festival Imbolc, meaning 'ewe's milk'. Christians consider the lamb a symbol of the resurrected Christ. In Europe, a black sheep is considered a sign of good luck.

IF SHEEP IS YOUR POWER ANIMAL

You are peaceful and humble. You provide warmth, love and security for your family and willingly sacrifice your own needs for their benefit. You value compassion and service. Those close to you experience your spontaneous outbursts of joy and learn from you how to enjoy simple pleasures. You love to celebrate new beginnings, like the first day of spring. You are a source of comfort and solace when death is imminent, because you understand journey of the soul in the afterlife.

ASK SHEEP TO HELP YOU

- Be more expressive of your emotions, especially joy and happiness
- Enjoy everyday pleasures, such as a good meal or a beautiful sunset
- Put your education and skills to work in service of others
- Accept love and protection from others

ACCESS SHEEP'S POWER BY

- Healing any wounds from the past with help from a therapist or counsellor
- Purifying any negative feelings you have towards family members by forgiving them

The Ancient Egyptians kept sheep for their meat, milk, hide and wool. They used flocks of sheep to trample seeds into their fields. How can you make sure the positive seeds you sow, in your work and family life, will take root and grow?

As a dream symbol
Masculinity, force, intelligence, creativity, new beginning, vision

As a guardian or protector
Protects new creative projects
Guards intellectual property

As a healer
Heals low energy
Helps you start over in life

As an oracle or omen
Act on your ideas
Assert yourself

RAM

MYTHS AND STORIES

For ancient Greeks and Romans, the spiral horns of the ram were symbols of enlightenment. The ram is also associated with the Roman god Mars and strength in combat.

IF RAM IS YOUR POWER ANIMAL

You are highly intelligent and have a very active imagination. You require constant external stimulation to feed your voracious mind. You have the power to inspire and initiate many creative projects. Those in your circle see you as powerful, charismatic and visionary. You are not afraid to tackle situations 'head on,' but do so impulsively, without much forethought. In your best aspect, you spiritually inspire; at your worst, you can be very aggressive and blind to others' needs.

ASK RAM TO HELP YOU

- Integrate your masculine and feminine sides, symbolized by his forceful masculinity and the femininity of his beautiful spiral horns
- Be less combative and more sensitive to your family and colleagues

ACCESS RAM'S POWER BY

- Imagining the great spiral horns sprouting from your own intelligent head and writing down any creative ideas that emerge
- Envisaging the best future for yourself, your nation and the world

The ram can find purchase on 5 cm (2 in) of a trail ledge and can leap from them over spans up to 6 m (20 ft) wide. How can you make the leap from small, nascent ideas, or tiny openings, to successful endeavours?

INTERPRETATION GUIDE

As a dream symbol
Abundance, prosperity, generosity,
fertility, intelligence, affection

As a guardian or protector
Protects wealth
Guards against greed

As a healer
Roots out infection
Heals through relationship
with earth

As an oracle or omen
Prepare for a financial windfall
Avoid overindulgence

PIG

MYTHS AND STORIES

The Greek goddess Demeter, also known as Porcis the Sow, carried a little pig under her arm. The Tantric Buddhist goddess Marici, the Diamond Sow, sits on a lotus flower supported by nine pigs.

IF PIG IS YOUR POWER ANIMAL

You are highly intelligent, affectionate and independent. You love children and large families. As a parent, you are extremely giving. Most find you sweet, innocent and good-natured, but you can be fierce when you need to be. You have a keen sense of smell and appreciate the best in life: truffles, chocolate and champagne suit your taste. You are wealthier than average. When negative, you are greedy and demand more than your share. For you, the earth holds the deepest wisdom. You have been known to predict the future.

ASK PIG TO HELP YOU

• Integrate your high intelligence, sensuality, family life and career

• Stop worrying about money and have faith that you will always have enough

• Approach your life with a sense of ease

ACCESS PIG'S POWER BY

• Validating and honouring both emotional and cerebral intelligence

• Making room for abundance in your life

• Enjoying the luxuries of life, such as expensive wines and foods, without guilt

---

Lyall Watson, field naturalist and author of the book The Whole Hog *(Profile Books, 2004), maintains that pigs are more intelligent then we think. Likewise, we often disregard how intelligent we are. List ten aspects of your intelligence in your journal.*

As a dream symbol
Strategy, appearances, wit, wisdom, equilibrium, maternal instinct

As a guardian or protector
Protects you when you are under stress
Maintains your emotional equilibrium

As a healer
Heals mineral deficiencies
Promotes emotional and mental stability

As an oracle or omen
Things are not as they appear
Be more strategic in your approach

OPOSSUM

MYTHS AND STORIES
Early European explorers described the unfamiliar American opossum as having the head of a pig, the tail of a rat, the size of a cat and a pouch for carrying and suckling babies.

IF OPOSSUM IS YOUR POWER ANIMAL
When you listen to others, you instinctively know what is true and what is false. You manage threatening situations using your keen instinct, intelligence and wit. If needs be, you will appear weak and submissive or, if called for, you 'bare your teeth' and threaten to attack. Both are simple strategies that you employ at the drop of a hat. Your goal in any situation is to live and let live, avoiding hurt to yourself or others. Your friends are impressed by your emotional equilibrium and lack of ego. You are a master of disguise and appearance and could probably be successful in the theatre. If female, you are an exceptionally loving and protective mother.

ASK OPOSSUM TO HELP YOU
- Assess any situation and react appropriately
- Use appearance and surprise to further your goals

ACCESS OPOSSUM'S POWER BY
- If you are a new parent, carrying your baby in a pouch-like carrier in front of you
- Pretending to be dead as a defence
- Wearing musk essential oil

Opossums avoid a fight by feigning death. Playing dead in the face of aggression allows for new energy and a creative solution. What happens when you abruptly give in during a fight? How can this transform a negative situation?

As a dream symbol
Dexterity, adaptability, generosity,
opportunism, playfulness, theft

As a guardian or protector
Protects the underdog
Guards against deception

As a healer
Recommends mineral baths
Heals with cleansing herbs

As an oracle or omen
Be aware of takers
Provide for your own needs first

RACOON

MYTHS AND STORIES

According to a Native American legend, the racoon received its facemask because he played a trick on his coyote friend. The angry coyote threw him into a fire. He soon felt remorse, dowsed the racoon with white mud, but neglected the charred fur around his eyes.

IF RACOON IS YOUR POWER ANIMAL

You have great manual dexterity that serves you when you paint or play a musical instrument. You may be a political activist, dedicated to helping the elderly, the poor and those not able to care for themselves. When you raise funds for various social causes, your friends call you Robin Hood, because you are good at convincing the rich to part with their money. Ever resourceful, you always have what you need in life. You love to play with your appearance and take

on different personas. You may even enjoy amateur dramatics. In your negative aspect, you can become a thief of possessions or ideas.

ASK RACOON TO HELP YOU

- Practise generosity in all areas of your life
- Recognize opportunities
- Be more adaptable and playful

ACCESS RACOON'S POWER BY

- Taking apart an old clock to increase manual dexterity
- Playing with masks and disguises

The racoon is known for its unique masked face markings. Masks have been used all over the world to achieve altered states and explore knowledge hidden from the conscious mind. Create and wear a mask of your own personal power animal.

As a dream symbol
Scattered energy, prudence, preparedness, bravery, enthusiasm, hoarding

As a guardian or protector
Defends your neighbourhood
Warns of the approach of an adversary

As a healer
Helps you manage energy
Promotes better self-care

As an oracle or omen
Get rid of clutter
Be more focused

SQUIRREL

MYTHS AND STORIES

The squirrel appears on the walls of Mayan ruins and was associated with the Mayan king's responsibility to maintain stores of grain to feed his people.

IF SQUIRREL IS YOUR POWER ANIMAL

You gather and store energy and ideas, as well as money and things. Perhaps you are a researcher or a news reporter. Your sociable nature makes you a good media person. You are an excellent planner, but not good at completing what you start. When you go on holiday you pack extra clothes, 'just in case'. Your car has a first-aid kit and you always carry a penknife. In a nutshell, you are always prepared for any contingency. In your negative aspect you become a hoarder or a nag or an insufferable critic, always expecting the worst. Your erratic behaviour gets on others' nerves. When in balance, you are cheerful, practical, energetic and generous.

ASK SQUIRREL TO HELP YOU

- Make sure you will have enough money for retirement
- Balance gathering and releasing your money and possessions

ACCESS SQUIRREL'S POWER BY

- Playing 'hide and seek' with your kids and hiding behind trees
- Holding a car-boot or garage sale for the things you no longer need

Squirrels store seeds and nuts in the ground, or under fallen leaves, so they can retrieve them during the long, cold winter. If you have gathered many ideas and possessions over time, look them over to see if they are still useful to you.

INTERPRETATION GUIDE

As a dream symbol
Fear, fertility, moon, wit, humility, leaps, creativity, softness

As a guardian or protector
Guards against excessive worry

As a healer
Heals phobias
Soothes nerves

As an oracle or omen
Don't let fearful thoughts reproduce
Look for the hidden teaching in experiences

RABBIT

MYTHS AND STORIES

The origin of the Easter bunny is found in a Teutonic legend. The rabbit was once a bird but was transformed into its present form by Eostra, the goddess of spring. In gratitude, the rabbit laid eggs.

IF RABBIT IS YOUR POWER ANIMAL

You have a problem with fear. The very things you dread most – bankruptcy, divorce, serious illness, losing your job, physical attack – may appear in your life because your fearful energy attracts them. When misfortune does strike, you become paralyzed. When you realize fear is a mental state, your life improves by leaps and bounds. It is then your love of life emerges, allowing you to grace the world with your sweetness and very fertile, creative mind. You believe in magic and the fairy world and sometimes see fairies in your garden at dusk. You are keenly aware of the phases of the moon. When not afraid, your generosity knows no bounds.

ASK RABBIT TO HELP YOU

- Realize life is short and enjoy it to the full
- Get pregnant
- Be quick to avoid potential disaster
- Make the leap into a new career

ACCESS RABBIT'S POWER BY

- Tracking the moon and noting how its phases affect you
- Spending time in your garden at dusk

___

In many cultures the rabbit is associated with the moon because baby rabbits take about a month to mature. When the moon is waxing start new projects; when it is waning banish things you no longer want in your life.

___

As a dream symbol
Playfulness, innocence, humility, faith,
trust, wonder, protection

As a guardian or protector
Protects your 'inner child'
Guards against physical or
verbal attack

As a healer
Heals through dance
Promotes relaxation and play

As an oracle or omen
Be aware of a possible confrontation
Open to childlike fantasy

PORCUPINE

MYTHS AND STORIES

The Algonquin goddess Norwan also
has the name Hluyuk Tikimit. This means
'dancing porcupine'.

IF PORCUPINE IS YOUR POWER ANIMAL

You are an easy-going, gentle person, who
enjoys life. Your positive, hopeful and playful
nature endears you to others. They rely on
you to remain calm in the most stressful
situations. You trust easily and are
trustworthy. You believe life has a higher
purpose and you live according to your
spiritual values. You are careful to warn
others when they are intrusive and you
will do anything to avoid a conflict. But,
when pushed to your limits, you can cause
deep, stinging and long-lasting wounds with
your words.

ASK PORCUPINE TO HELP YOU

- Heal from a failed relationship
- Defend yourself, if you need to, without
  being aggressive
- Trust others so as to create the opening
  for others to love you in return
- Open your heart to those people you
  find difficult

ACCESS PORCUPINE'S POWER BY

- Walking through a park or wooded area
  and generating positive feelings toward
  any birds or animals you may encounter
- Playing a game with a child

---

*Contrary to popular belief, the porcupine does not
'shoot' his quills. Rather, he backs up toward his
attacker and swipes his tail, dislodging the barbs
into them. Learn ways to communicate better, in
order to avoid painful, angry confrontations.*

As a dream symbol
Protection, stability, benevolence, self-reliance, home, steadiness

As a guardian or protector
Protects against becoming enmeshed in others' problems
Guards against physical, verbal and psychic attack

As a healer
Promotes longevity
Helps you metabolize vitamin D

As an oracle or omen
Withdraw from bad situations
Honour your own pace

TURTLE OR TORTOISE

MYTHS AND STORIES

The Native American Huron tribe believed the world was built on the turtle's back and referred to the landmass of the Americas as 'Turtle Island'. Both the Chinese and Hindus also believed the turtle supported the world.

IF TURTLE IS YOUR POWER ANIMAL

You are a very old soul and others turn to you for your wisdom and compassion. You are slow-paced, but strong, steady and reliable. You are extremely sensitive to your environment and can even perceive auras and energy fields. When travelling with friends you are the navigator and map-reader. Nothing escapes your keen awareness and deep understanding of everything that is going on around you. In your negative aspect, you withdraw 'into your shell' to avoid responsibility.

ASK TURTLE TO HELP YOU

- Incubate and mature your creative ideas before exposing them to others
- Be selective about what you read or view, especially on television or the internet
- Protect yourself from negative energy
- Adapt to changes outside of your control

ACCESS TURTLE'S POWER BY

- Studying ancient Buddhist, Hindu, Greek and Native American wisdom
- Enclosing yourself in a small dark closet or space and noting how that feels

Baby turtles must be extremely self-reliant, as female turtles lay their eggs in sand or earth and leave their young to fend for themselves. Try to find the middle ground between being overly dependent on others and being too self-reliant.

As a dream symbol
Wisdom, creativity, networking,
communication, entrapment, balance

As a guardian or protector
Protects from entangling situations
Guards against materialism

As a healer
Helps assimilate negative experiences
Closes and heals surgical incisions

As an oracle or omen
Watch for entrapment
Honour the sacred as feminine

SPIDER

MYTHS AND STORIES

In Hindu lore the spider symbolizes the goddess Maya, the weaver of illusion. The Native American goddess Spider Woman is considered the weaver of the universe and the creator of the first alphabet. Many stories identify the spider as a symbol of the sacred feminine.

IF SPIDER IS YOUR POWER ANIMAL

You may make your living creating illusion – perhaps in advertising, fashion or theatre. Or you may work as a writer or as a website designer. Creativity is your consuming passion. For you, the world is an inter-dependent and interconnected web of vibrating energy. You may play with illusion, but, as a spiritual seeker, you try to understand the true meaning of life. Relationships come and go, but you prefer to remain independent. You have a refined and delicate appearance that belies a powerful and intimidating personality. When angered, you move like lightning to attack and in doing so, devastate your opponent.

ASK SPIDER TO HELP YOU

- Experience reality as pulsating energy
- Weave the various parts of your life into an integrated whole
- Bring form and structure to your ideas

ACCESS SPIDER'S POWER BY

- Watching a spider in her web
- Sending an email to five friends

The spider's silk is produced as a liquid within its silk glands and emerges from its body as solid silk fibres. Think about how your thoughts and actions manifest solid realities in the external world.

INTERPRETATION GUIDE

As a dream symbol
Wisdom, potential, awakening,
transmutation, initiation, resurrection,
rebirth

As a guardian or protector
Guards sacred mysteries
Protects spiritual seekers

As a healer
Clears and awakens chakras
Purifies toxicity that could cause illness

As an oracle or omen
Be more flexible
Shed what is holding you back

SNAKE

MYTHS AND STORIES

The Dogon people of Mali believed the snake taught humans how to give birth. The Hindu goddess Kali is shown wearing a necklace of snakes, a symbol of her *kundalini* power (see page 8). The Medusa, an ancient Greek goddess, has hissing snakes for hair.

IF SNAKE IS YOUR POWER ANIMAL

You have the capacity to grow as a person because you are not afraid to shed ideas or relationships that no longer serve you. Like an alchemist, you transmute negative experiences – a bad business deal, a car accident or a serious illness – into positive spiritual lessons. You have a keen sense of smell and can 'smell' danger before it arrives. When you observe others, you see their heart and soul. You have an intense, charismatic personality. As a teacher, you help others access higher states of consciousness.

ASK SNAKE TO HELP YOU

- Transform anything in your life that has become stagnant
- Grow in spiritual knowledge
- Confront fear of change or loss

ACCESS SNAKE'S POWER BY

- Observing and learning about snakes
- Helping your spine be more flexible by taking a yoga class

The snake as your power animal can devour those things you no longer want. Offer to the snake any negative habit, such as smoking or overeating, that you would like to remove from your life.

INTERPRETATION GUIDE

As a dream symbol
Regeneration, instinct, subtlety, intuition, detachment, endurance

As a guardian or protector
Defends against psychological manipulation
Protects through emotional detachment

As a healer
Heals through energy
Heals through dreams

As an oracle or omen
Pay attention to your dreams
Be aware of physical and emotional responses from your gut

LIZARD

MYTHS AND STORIES
In Native American cultures the lizard was seen as a visionary and an illuminator of the soul. In Hawaii the lizard is revered as an *aumakua* or guardian spirit.

IF LIZARD IS YOUR POWER ANIMAL
You are clairsentient, that is, capable of sensing beyond a normal sensory range. You hear, smell and see, but also pick up subtle energies. For example, you may feel sick around someone having negative thoughts about you. You are shy and sometimes experience loneliness. Because of your acute sensitivity, you have developed a protective shield that keeps you from opening your heart to others. You sometimes inflate your importance as a defence. Others may see you as lazy, but you can move with lightning speed once you are motivated or inspired.

You are willing to endure hardship to gain spiritual knowledge, perhaps through fasting.

ASK LIZARD TO HELP YOU
- Become detached from other's opinions
- Rely on your dreams for guidance
- Get more in touch with your intuition

ACCESS LIZARD'S POWER BY
- Starting a dream journal and recording your dreams nightly
- Rubbing your hands together, then holding them 2.5 cm (1 in) apart to feel the energy generated

When a predator attacks a lizard, the lizard cleverly escapes by detaching its tail. Magically, it regenerates a new one. Can you let go of behaviour and relationships that no longer serve you to make room for new growth?

As a dream symbol
Stealth, prudence, ambition, intelligence, deceit, prosperity

As a guardian or protector
Shelters new beginnings
Defends against negativity

As a healer
Heals damaged self-esteem
Transforms aggression and greed

As an oracle or omen
Don't be a 'pack rat'
Watch for betrayal

RAT

MYTHS AND STORIES

In Hinduism the rat represents foresight and prudence and is the vehicle of Ganesh, the elephant-headed god of wisdom, prosperity and successful endeavours. The rat is the first of the 12 animals of the Chinese zodiac. In Japan the white rat is the symbol of Daikoku, the god of prosperity.

IF RAT IS YOUR POWER ANIMAL

You are ingenious, charming, resourceful and generous to those you love. You channel your restless, nervous energy into hard work. Because you are a shrewd businessperson you are financially well off. You are alert, persevering, perfectionist, easy to anger and full of ambition. Family life is important to you and you enjoy a large circle of friends. The opposite sex finds you irresistible. In your negative aspect, you can be vicious, aggressive and cunning. You can hoard out of fear of not having enough.

ASK RAT TO HELP YOU

- Know beforehand if someone is going to betray or deceive you
- Manage your finances
- Reduce your tendency to be lazy

ACCESS RAT'S POWER BY

- Buying stock in a new company
- Starting a stamp, coin or other collection
- Entering a room without anyone noticing

Rats live in large groups, *with certain rats dominating and controlling the others. Are you more comfortable in hierarchical groups or families with one strong person at the head? Or do you prefer a more egalitarian, democratic arrangement?*

As a dream symbol
Introspection, invisibility, humility,
destruction, simplicity,
gentleness, detail

As a guardian or protector
Protects you when signing a contract
Guards through invisibility

As a healer
Promotes trust in the Divine
Enables better mental concentration

As an oracle or omen
Take advantage of small openings
Be more aware of others' needs

MOUSE

MYTHS AND STORIES

As late as 1822, offerings of gold and silver mice were left at the shrine of St Gertrude of Nivelles in Cologne. Mice represented souls in Purgatory, to whom the saint had a great devotion.

IF MOUSE IS YOUR POWER ANIMAL

You have exceptional organizational skills and delight in the smallest details. Perhaps you are a professional organizer, an accountant or a librarian. In some areas you are fastidious, but in others you are less so. For example, you may keep a perfect house, but neglect your appearance. Because you intently focus on what is in front of you, you have trouble seeing the big picture. Although you are never malicious, you can be destructive because of ignorance of the effect of your actions. You have tremendous trust and faith in a higher power. Others admire you for your gentleness and humility, but could do without your constant fussing over minutiae.

ASK MOUSE TO HELP YOU

- Realize the fleeting, vulnerable quality of life
- File the papers on your desk
- Pay more attention to people and your surroundings

ACCESS MOUSE'S POWER BY

- Lying on your belly in the grass and experiencing a mouse's view of the world
- Cleaning and organizing a closet

Mice have sharp front teeth that are used for chewing things into small pieces. The mouse's secret for happy living is, therefore, if you have a problem, break it into small pieces and handle them one at a time.

INTERPRETATION GUIDE

As a dream symbol
Loyalty, service, protection, compassion, tolerance, companionship

As a guardian or protector
Guards your home and property
Rescues you from dangerous situations

As a healer
Heals the heart
Detects latent cancer and heart disease

As an oracle or omen
Be more playful with friends
Protect your home

DOG

MYTHS AND STORIES

The Egyptian dog, Anubis, was associated with the underworld. Artemis, Greek Goddess of the hunt, known as Diana in Roman mythology, kept a pack of 50 dogs.

IF DOG IS YOUR POWER ANIMAL

You may be in a service profession – a doctor, therapist, counsellor, nurse or minister. If not, you are the one your family and friends turn to when they are suffering or in need of advice. Love, loyalty and commitment are your core qualities and deepest values. For you, marriage is an unbreakable union and faithfulness is a given. If you have a weakness, it is that you have a tendency to be codependent. Because of this, you struggle to be respectful of your own needs when in relationship to others. You are happiest in the company of friends and family and most comfortable when under the protection of a strong leader.

ASK DOG TO HELP YOU

- Learn to love unconditionally
- Set and communicate clear boundaries with others
- Pursue your desires with enthusiasm
- Balance your needs with those of others

ACCESS DOG'S POWER BY

- Being aware of and attentive to your partner's mood
- Volunteering at a dog shelter
- Renewing your marriage vows

If you want a dog as a pet, consider adopting from a pet shelter. Spend time choosing your companion and make your choice based on the emotional connection you feel in his or her presence.

As a dream symbol
Mystery, mothering, independence, curiosity, self-absorption, ease, playfulness

As a guardian or protector
Protects women and children
Guards against home fires

As a healer
Detoxifies through its energy field
Heals loneliness

As an oracle or omen
Good or bad luck
Is there a predator in your life?

CAT

MYTHS AND STORIES
Bast, the cat-headed Egyptian goddess, is the protector of cats, women and children. In European lore the cat is the witch's familiar or power animal that helps her enter other dimensions.

IF CAT IS YOUR POWER ANIMAL
You either fascinate or repel. People rarely have a neutral opinion about you. Nocturnal by nature, you do your best creative work after dark. Many find you aloof and self-absorbed, but if they are willing to burn the midnight oil they might find you to be a lot more fun. After dark you love to play games, listen to music and sing. You are seductive, but those you attract find you frustratingly hard to get. You are definitely picky about what you eat and can change your mind about anything at the drop of a hat. Others would do well to learn from your ability to deeply relax and meditate. At those times you enter deeper spiritual states with ease.

ASK CAT TO HELP YOU
- Get rid of all tension in your body
- Become more self-possessed
- Love yourself

ACCESS CAT'S POWER BY
- Taking a nap in a sunspot on the floor
- Staying up all night
- Buying sexy underwear

A cat's meow can express a range of emotions from curiosity to hunger, from irritation to loneliness. Studies have determined that a cat can make more than 60 different sounds. How expressive is the sound of your voice?

As a dream symbol
Power, sensuality, passion, adventure, mysticism, aggression, sensitivity

As a guardian or protector
Protects your integrity
Guards against fear

As a healer
Heals fear and timidity
Promotes a strong constitution

As an oracle or omen
Powerful spiritual realizations
Prosperity is around the corner

TIGER

MYTHS AND STORIES

The Chinese god of wealth, Tsai Shen Yeh, is depicted sitting on a tiger. The tiger is sacred to the wrathful Hindu goddess Durga.

IF TIGER IS YOUR POWER ANIMAL

You are bold, adventurous, strong and courageous. You are exciting and exhilarating to be around and you command great respect for your power. Leadership comes naturally to you but, unfortunately, you are rarely a good boss. Your short temper makes life difficult for your employees and your impulsiveness can harm your bottom line. If there is anything that sets you apart from others, it is your fearless love of excitement. Risk-taking is in your blood. Activities that scare most people, like bungee-jumping or skydiving, attract you. When not angry, you are a sensitive and sympathetic listener. You are a very sensual and sexual person, but prefer to remain single. When alone, you enjoy pondering the mysteries of the universe.

ASK TIGER TO HELP YOU

- Take more risks in business and love
- Validate the power and strength you have
- Get what you want

ACCESS TIGER'S POWER BY

- Reading William Blake's poem *The Tyger*
- Volunteering to help protect the wild tiger in India

The tiger, the largest of all cats, can reach an impressive 4 m (13 ft) in length and 300 kg (650 lb) in weight. Do you find yourself intimidated, inspired, jealous or admiring of powerful people? Meditate on the tiger to understand how you relate to power.

As a dream symbol
Assertiveness, authority, cooperation, pride, imagination, power

As a guardian or protector
Defends important buildings and institutions
Protects the family unit

As a healer
Balances the elements (fire, water, earth, air) in your body
Heals through heat and sunlight

As an oracle or omen
Bring discipline to your life
You are your own authority

LION

MYTHS AND STORIES

The Buddha is depicted seated on a lotus throne supported by eight lions. Sekhmet, the lion-headed Egyptian goddess, bears the image of the sun on her head.

IF LION IS YOUR POWER ANIMAL

You are a true family person and an indulgent and loving parent. If male, you probably are not the best provider, but you are a strong protector. Perhaps you are a stay-at-home dad. Your family feels extremely safe in your powerful presence. If female, you may work outside the home in a high-powered job. Neither of you like confrontations and will avoid them at all cost. However, if threatened, you literally terrify your opponent. Although you have an imposing and powerful persona, you prefer to rely on a disciplined mind as the ultimate key to success. To this end, you increase your focus and concentration through meditation, affirmations and visualizations.

ASK LION TO HELP YOU

- Validate feminine power and energy
- Gain strength through discipline over negative impulses
- Be a more loving and attentive parent

ACCESS LION'S POWER BY

- Studying the astrological sign Leo
- Exploring meditation or martial arts

The Tarot card Strength depicts a woman subduing a lion, demonstrating that inner strength is more powerful than raw physical power. Have you ever relied on your inner strength rather than anger and aggression to deal with a difficult problem?

As a dream symbol
Memory, grace, strength, emotion,
intelligence, royalty, sexual power

As a guardian or protector
Protects your extended family
Guards against obstacles to success
in business

As a healer
Heals ruptures in family or community
Fosters peace and tranquillity

As an oracle or omen
Prosperous new beginning
Follow your heart

ELEPHANT

MYTHS AND STORIES

Ganesh, the elephant-headed son of the
Hindu god Shiva, is the deity of new
beginnings, the Lord of Success and the
destroyer of all obstacles.

IF ELEPHANT IS YOUR POWER ANIMAL

You stand strong in yourself and command
great respect from others – for your grace,
intelligence, gentle power and regal bearing.
If you are a woman, you love bringing
together the female children, mothers and
matriarchs in your family to cook and share
stories. After a long, hot day, you crave a
soothing bath or dip in the pool. If you are
male, you are a bit of a rogue. You have a
reputation for your powerful sexual drive
that may have, at some point, landed you in
trouble. Whether male or female, you have
an acute sense of smell and can discern

when a situation 'smells bad.' Your driving
concerns are for the care of children, respect
for the elderly and adequate health care for all.

ASK ELEPHANT TO HELP YOU

- Process traumatic memories
- Renew family ties
- Begin a new project

ACCESS ELEPHANT'S POWER BY

- Having a party for the eldest female in
  your family
- Visiting an elephant in the wild or nearest
  safari park

Elephants are called pachyderms – *a Greek word
meaning 'thick-skinned'. Yet their skin is tender
enough to feel insect bites. How can you have a
'thick skin' when you need to protect yourself, but
also be open and sensitive to others?*

INTERPRETATION GUIDE

As a dream symbol
Perspective, gentleness, heart connection, silence, compassion, third eye, foresight

As a guardian or protector
Protects from unseen danger
Guards against myopic thinking

As a healer
Heals hypertension
Promotes correct body alignment

As an oracle or omen
Pay more attention to body language
Stretch for what you want

GIRAFFE

MYTHS AND STORIES

In an African tale, God asked the giraffe if it had a special wish. The giraffe said, 'Lord, my wish is to have wisdom.' God answered, 'And so you will never speak, for talkative people are fools, but silence is wisdom.'

IF GIRAFFE IS YOUR POWER ANIMAL

You are able to look at problems from all sides and practise equanimity in all your affairs. Your unique perspective is simultaneously spiritual and practical, visionary and grounded. You have a very big heart and you willingly offer it to others. When friends are in trouble – marriage falling apart or losing a job – they always turn to you. Your sensitivity, intelligence and amazing grace delight your friends and life partner. Because you have the gift of foresight, you excel at divination, astrology and fortune-telling. You

prefer to live in a family or group where everyone has equal power and input.

ASK GIRAFFE TO HELP YOU

- Connect your head and heart
- Keep your focus on your higher goals
- Practise standing tall both mentally and physically

ACCESS GIRAFFE'S POWER BY

- Standing in a high place and surveying your surroundings
- Imagining what your life may be like one year from now

A giraffe is basically a silent animal, though it can utter a few soft sounds. Silence is valued by many spiritual traditions as a way to calm the mind. As an experiment, try refraining from using your voice for 24 hours.

INTERPRETATION GUIDE

As a dream symbol
Power, integrity, impeccability, sacrifice, shadow, potential

As a guardian or protector
Protects you when travelling at night
Helps maintain your integrity

As a healer
Helps you reclaim your power
Heals using phases of the moon

As an oracle or omen
Move beyond fear of the unknown
Danger arriving in a beautiful package

JAGUAR

MYTHS AND STORIES

The jaguar was the most revered animal in Meso-American culture. Mayan kings adorned themselves with jaguar skins and necklaces of jaguar teeth.

IF JAGUAR IS YOUR POWER ANIMAL

You love being around water and enjoy swimming. Whenever you can get away, you spend time in tropical locations. You have a powerful and intense personality and those who don't know you may find you a little scary. Your preoccupation with the shadow or the negative aspects of the psyche adds to your mystique. But, rather than being perverse, your interest in the shadow is a sign of your compassion and your desire to help others. Acknowledging your shadow aspects – your greed, lust and desire for power – leads to your own healing and maturation. Your honesty, integrity and impeccable ethical standards are an inspiration for others.

ASK JAGUAR TO HELP YOU

- Do your best at all times
- Give up the desire to control others
- Be true to yourself
- Sacrifice comfortable illusion for hard truth

ACCESS JAGUAR'S POWER BY

- Reviewing the values and ethics that inform your life
- Noticing any negativity you project on others and seeing if it applies to yourself

---

Jaguars are the third largest cats in the world, after tigers and lions. For the ancient Mayan Indians of South America, the jaguar symbolized great power and courage. Do you need courage to quit your job or to leave a bad relationship?

INTERPRETATION GUIDE

As a dream symbol
Beauty, femininity, darkness, power, passion, rebirth, redemption

As a guardian or protector
Protects when confronting a painful past
Functions as a permanent protector and guardian

As a healer
Helps you reclaim power taken from you
Helps you reclaim power you gave away

As an oracle or omen
Pursue spiritual enlightenment
A loss will lead to something better

PANTHER

MYTHS AND STORIES

In many cultures the panther is the symbol of the feminine, the dark mother goddess, magic, power and the dark of the moon.

IF PANTHER IS YOUR POWER ANIMAL

When you have problems they are very serious. Addiction, unhealed child abuse, a failed marriage or trouble with the law may figure in your history. The good news is that, no matter how terrible or degrading your past, you will emerge a stronger person, in touch with your great and true power. At some point in your life you will experience redemption and rebirth leading to a spiritual awakening. Your problems stem from not knowing how powerful you are and how to channel that power toward positive ends. Dark, passionate and striking in appearance, you have no trouble attracting men or women.

ASK PANTHER TO HELP YOU

- Overcome a serious personal problem
- Get in touch with your true power
- Be comfortable with the unknown
- Have faith that your life can be transformed

ACCESS PANTHER'S POWER BY

- Mentoring troubled teenagers
- Seeking out a spiritual teacher
- Dressing in black velvet

The panther will often retreat to sleep in a cave for several days. If you have had a difficult experience or trauma, take a few days to recharge your batteries, heal your emotional wounds and get restful sleep.

INTERPRETATION GUIDE

As a dream symbol
Playfulness, spontaneity, imagination, foolishness, ingenuity, selflessness

As a guardian or protector
Protects family warmth and closeness
Guards against evil

As a healer
Promotes laughter as medicine
Encourages effortless, tension-free movement

As an oracle or omen
Good health
Success in anything you do

MONKEY

MYTHS AND STORIES

One of the most popular Hindu deities is Hanuman, the monkey god, known for his courage, perseverance, selflessness and devotion.

IF MONKEY IS YOUR POWER ANIMAL

You are highly intelligent, sociable and well liked. You are unpredictable and never boring. When you are around, friends know to expect the unexpected. At work you are quick and clever and can improvise when needed to meet your objectives. When there is a problem you have the ability to examine it from all directions and suggest the best solution. When thinking of you, the word 'fun' comes to mind, as you are very playful. You don't mind making a fool of yourself if it makes people laugh. You like to be close and physically affectionate with family members and friends. If someone is in need, you make yourself available to help. When negative, you can be silly, inappropriate and irritating.

ASK MONKEY TO HELP YOU

- Be less serious and more playful
- Be more devoted to your family
- Move with a more fluid motion

ACCESS MONKEY'S POWER BY

- Taking a class in gymnastics or swinging on a playground jungle gym
- Eating tropical fruit

Social grooming helps maintain closeness in monkey families. In grooming, one monkey picks over and cleans the other's fur, and both seem to find this enjoyable. Encourage closeness with members of your family by trading head massages.

INTERPRETATION GUIDE

As a dream symbol
Integration, digestion, danger, survival, aggression, fecundity, power

As a guardian or protector
Protects against rash judgements and half-baked solutions
Warns against rigidity and inflexibility

As a healer
Strengthens adrenal system, aids in everyday survival
Promotes good digestion and metabolism

As an oracle or omen
What is the missing piece in your life?

ALLIGATOR OR CROCODILE

MYTHS AND STORIES

In Egypt, the crocodile was a symbol of chaos and is associated with the god Set.

IF ALLIGATOR OR CROCODILE IS YOUR POWER ANIMAL

You are a very ancient soul and an extremely powerful person. You are so powerful that you can wreak havoc if your negative tendencies get out of control. In your worst aspect you feel entitled to anything you want and will aggressively and ruthlessly pursue it regardless of the consequences. That said, you have many wonderful qualities that others might well emulate. For example, you are a consummate survivor and nothing keeps you down for long. When making a difficult decision you know how to digest the facts, take your time and come to the right conclusion. You are a master of timing, whether in business or romance.

ASK ALLIGATOR OR CROCODILE TO HELP YOU

- Pursue what you want in life
- Control your aggressive instincts
- Consider the effect of your actions on others when pursuing your goals

ACCESS ALLIGATOR'S OR CROCODILE'S POWER BY

- Giving yourself a month to mull over an important decision
- Carefully observing your business competitor before making your move

Like the legendary dragon, alligators and crocodiles are said to be keepers of knowledge and wisdom. What wisdom and knowledge do you embody? Write a few pages in your journal about what you have learned about life to date.

As a dream symbol
Transformation, healing, hallucination,
renewal, transcendence, poison

As a guardian or protector
Guards against poisoning
Sustains during transitions

As a healer
Helps you recover from ingesting toxins
Heals through detoxification diet

As an oracle or omen
Good fortune is coming your way
Jump from the material to the spiritual

FROG

MYTHS AND STORIES

The Egyptian goddess Heket was portrayed as a frog. She was the sacred midwife of mothers and newborns.

IF FROG IS YOUR POWER ANIMAL

You are adaptable in times of change. Where others might falter, you can hit the ground running. You love water and enjoy swimming. Your friends and co-workers complain that you are remote and unavailable. Actually, you are just quiet and self-contained. You are always in touch with how you feel. In fact, although you appear aloof, you are quite sensitive to the feelings of others. Your creativity inspires your co-workers. When you appear in a room, any negativity evaporates. When negative, you can get stuck in the mud, become stagnant and refuse to let go of those things that no longer support you.

ASK FROG TO HELP YOU

- Cry freely to release pent-up emotions
- Heal yourself by facing those things in you that you find ugly or unacceptable
- Cleanse yourself of situations that no longer work for you

ACCESS FROG'S POWER BY

- Observing tadpoles transform into frogs
- Swimming in a lake or pond
- Listening to frogs croaking on a summer night

Male frogs use their voice to call females during the mating season. Females have a voice, but it is much quieter. Try singing softly to your partner or lover and see if it improves your relationship.

As a dream symbol
Work, faithfulness, organization, diligence, comfort, ingenuity, productivity

As a guardian or protector
Protects against home invasion by humans or animals
Guards wealth and savings

As a healer
Heals through better breathing
Heals dental problems

As an oracle or omen
Have an escape route
Make home repairs

BEAVER

MYTHS AND STORIES
Capa, the Beaver, is an animistic spirit of the Lakota tribe. He is regarded as the patron of hard work and domestic tranquillity.

IF BEAVER IS YOUR POWER ANIMAL
You are industrious and hardworking and may be a professional builder, an architect or an engineer. Most would say you are humble and unassuming. Your first priority is a safe, secure and comfortable home. Work, providing for your family and being a faithful spouse, define you. You excel at organization and planning and you believe structure and discipline are essential for any creative process. You have the ability to work with a team and complete projects on time. Others may think you are a workaholic, but you are actually well balanced. After work, you know how to relax and have fun with family and friends.

ASK BEAVER TO HELP YOU
- Make your environment comfortable and secure
- Be more disciplined and steady in your work
- Plan and organize a new project

ACCESS BEAVER'S POWER BY
- Playing in an amateur sports team
- Rearranging the furniture in your home to make it more comfortable

Beavers cleverly build their homes in dammed-up rivers, by creating dry, cosy lodges that can only be entered through the water. Do you feel safe and secure where you live? If not, work toward creating a safe home for yourself.

As a dream symbol
Emotions, power, depth, family, aggression, bullying

As a guardian or protector
Guards the family unit
Protects against being taken advantage of

As a healer
Heals problems with dry, cracking skin
Heals mental confusion and disorientation

As an oracle or omen
Expect an unmovable obstacle
Recognize abundance

HIPPOPOTAMUS

MYTHS AND STORIES

The Egyptian goddess of birth, Ta-Urt, is sometimes depicted with a hippo's body and a lioness's head. In this form, she is a ferocious protector of children and family.

IF HIPPOPOTAMUS IS YOUR POWER ANIMAL

You love group activities and are miserable if you find yourself home alone. When challenged you rarely back down. Your imposing size can be intimidating to others. As a writer or artist, you know how to fully immerse yourself in the creative process and are not afraid to delve into your emotions. Because you are very grounded, you can go deep yet never lose your grasp on reality. In your negative aspect you can bulldoze your way though a meeting, trampling over other people's ideas and projects.

ASK HIPPOPOTAMUS TO HELP YOU

- Face troubling emotions
- Take on a long-term creative project, such as writing a novel or making a quilt
- Organize a family homecoming

ACCESS HIPPOPOTAMUS'S POWER BY

- Holding your breath under water for as long as you can to build your strength and stamina
- Writing in your journal about the emotion you have most trouble expressing

The hippopotamus is the second largest mammal on earth. Its name means 'water horse', and it spends most of its time in water. Try spending more time in water, either by swimming or taking long soaks in your bathtub.

INTERPRETATION GUIDE

As a dream symbol
Communication, joy, speed, intelligence, play, breath, friendship

As a guardian or protector
Protects communication from interception
Guards against group discord

As a healer
Heals through rhythmic breathing
Develops healing through laughter

As an oracle or omen
Use your intellect and emotions
Practise compassion

DOLPHIN

MYTHS AND STORIES

The dolphin is associated with the Sumerian goddesses Ishtar and Astarte. Dolphins appear on ancient Celtic coins. Native Americans called them the keeper of the sacred breath of life.

IF DOLPHIN IS YOUR POWER ANIMAL

You have psychic skills and can communicate telepathically with animals. Others find you fun-loving and delightful because you know the value of play. For you, play and laughter provide you with an emotional release after a long week at work. Your energy is boundless and friends have trouble keeping up with you when on holiday or just out on the town. Because you understand and express your emotions freely, you would make a good therapist or counsellor. You are very social and you have found it hard to settle down in a committed relationship. Unfortunately, when you want to avoid difficult situations, you irritate others by turning everything into a joke.

ASK DOLPHIN TO HELP YOU

- Practise unconditional love
- Love and live your life to the fullest
- Be more playful and fun-loving

ACCESS DOLPHIN'S POWER BY

- Breathing deeply, holding your breath under water, then surfacing and exhaling explosively to release energy

In recent years, researchers have observed dolphins in captivity creating underwater rings of air for their own amusement. How can you be more playful in every moment of your life? No matter what you are doing, look for opportunities to have fun.

INTERPRETATION GUIDE

As a dream symbol
Song, resurrection, awakening, communication, strength, intelligence

As a guardian or protector
Insulates against harsh weather
Protects with intuition and awareness

As a healer
Heals through releasing the voice
Promotes feminine reproductive health

As an oracle or omen
Abundance is coming your way
You are protected

WHALE

MYTHS AND STORIES

Slavic and Arabian myths claim that four whales support the world. The Tlingit tribe of Alaska considered the orca whale an ancestral spirit.

IF WHALE IS YOUR POWER ANIMAL

You are a gentle and protective parent and will instinctively protect anyone in danger. You have very sensitive hearing and are possibly clairaudient. You love to study ancient history, myths and legends, and may teach or write about those subjects. You enjoy singing with others, in a choir or just over a few beers, as a way to connect and release emotion. You may live close to the ocean which is extremely important to your health and vitality. Whether you have a small or large body, you move gracefully and effortlessly. If faced with a serious crisis, you

not only handle it well, but also emerge a stronger, wiser person.

ASK WHALE TO HELP YOU

- Study ancient myths for wisdom you can apply to your life
- Protect yourself from all kinds of danger – from physical attack to identity theft

ACCESS WHALE'S POWER BY

- Singing in a choir
- Listening to recordings of whale songs
- Working to protect endangered whales around the world

Humpback whales communicate with complex and hauntingly beautiful 'songs'. During the mating season, the males sing the same song, which they will change over time. What 'song' are you singing with your life, and is it time to create a new one?

SHARK

MYTHS AND STORIES

The ancient Maya carved shark images on stone temples and monuments. Australian aboriginal people believed shark spirits helped create Earth. The Haida tribe of British Columbia revered the shark as a powerful totem.

IF SHARK IS YOUR POWER ANIMAL

In order to remain calm and centred you need time to yourself. If you don't have time alone, you can become irritable, anxious and even more aggressive in your behaviour. You are very sensitive to electromagnetic currents and have to be careful around computers. In business, you terrify your competitors because you can be cold-blooded, fearless and unpredictable. 'Don't take it personally,' you say; it is what comes naturally to you. On the other hand, you have powerful protective instincts and will fight to the death for those you love. When your ferocious power is channelled you can do much good.

ASK SHARK TO HELP YOU

- Refine your sensory abilities by paying attention to smells, sounds, textures
- Ward off those things that frighten you

ACCESS SHARK'S POWER BY

- Creating a personal ritual to drive off negative people and influences
- Taking shark cartilage supplements for bone health and cancer prevention

Sharks have a streamlined, rounded, torpedo-shaped body and can generate great bursts of speed when excited or going after prey. When deadlines are looming can you shift gears and attack your work with accelerated speed and efficiency?

INTERPRETATION GUIDE

As a dream symbol
Confidence, heritage, abundance,
struggle, determination, renewal, spirit

As a guardian or protector
Protects during journeys
Guards against getting lost

As a healer
Heals depression
Enhances fertility

As an oracle or omen
Review your goals
Focus on your destination

SALMON

MYTHS AND STORIES

Native American, Norse and Celtic cultures considered the salmon to be sacred. Eating salmon was thought to bring wisdom and spiritual knowledge.

IF SALMON IS YOUR POWER ANIMAL

You have solid bonds with your kin. Every five to seven years, you attend a big family reunion, which usually marks a cycle of new beginnings in your life. You are never afraid to swim against the mainstream, if that is what your vision dictates. You are determined, independent and rarely daunted by life's obstacles. Challenges excite and motivate you. You approach problems head on and bravely work through them to realize your dreams. If you become stressed, you know to back off, temporarily, from battling the currents of life. You have a keen interest in spiritual matters. You never doubt your life's path, which can irritate others who struggle to know theirs.

ASK SALMON TO HELP YOU

- Make a spiritual pilgrimage to a sacred site
- Be single-minded in achieving your goals
- Have the courage to live your life the way you want to

ACCESS SALMON'S POWER BY

- Swimming against the current in a river
- Research your family tree
- Making a journey to your place of birth

Salmon spawn during the summer months after swimming upstream as far as 3,200 km (2,000 miles) from the ocean to their place of birth. If possible, visit the house you lived in as a child and reflect on your life journey to date.

FISH

MYTHS AND STORIES

A pair of golden fishes is one of the eight auspicious symbols in Buddhism.

IF FISH IS YOUR POWER ANIMAL

You have a dynamic personality and are very comfortable with movement and change. For others who have more fixed personalities, you may appear to be in perpetual transition. You are happiest when you are free to live your life as you please. You love to analyze people and speculate on their motivations. Your dreams guide and inform your life and you will eagerly listen to those of your spouse or companion. You believe in everyone's ability to transform themselves, if they so choose, in whatever way they want. When you talk to friends and family they are surprised to find themselves revealing their hidden fears and desires. Prayer and meditation help you balance your active life.

ASK FISH TO HELP YOU

- Reveal unconscious motivations in yourself and others
- Be more active in your career
- Feel free to enjoy life to the full

ACCESS FISH'S POWER BY

- Swimming underwater in tandem with two friends
- Setting up a tropical fish tank in your home

One of the most dangerous fish to humans is the deadly stonefish, which weighs only a few kilos. The largest fish, the whale shark, weighs over 15 tonnes and is completely harmless. What in your past life seemed small and harmless but held hidden dangers?

INTERPRETATION GUIDE

As a dream symbol
Regeneration, camouflage, eccentricity, manual dexterity, changeability, shape-shifting

As a guardian or protector
Guards by using a smokescreen
Protects by moving fast away from danger

As a healer
Restores through creativity
Heals carpal tunnel syndrome

As an oracle or omen
Diversify your assets
Be more adaptable

OCTOPUS

MYTHS AND STORIES

Kanaloa is the Hawaiian god of the underworld who appears in the shape of an octopus. It is said he can teach magic.

IF OCTOPUS IS YOUR POWER ANIMAL

You are shy and timid among strangers, but have more confidence if you are in familiar territory – your own neighbourhood, home or office. You are intelligent and can be covert in your dealings with others. At a party you are capable of fading, at will, into virtual invisibility. Friends won't be able to remember exactly what you were wearing. They will, however, remember that you are an eccentric dresser. Your changeability irritates co-workers who rely on you. You may pretend to be powerful, but those close to you are protective of you because they know you are emotionally and physically vulnerable. You are exceptionally gifted when it comes to using your hands. However, if you are male, you may have a problem keeping your hands to yourself.

ASK OCTOPUS TO HELP YOU

- Regenerate your business after a loss
- Acknowledge and accept your vulnerabilities

ACCESS OCTOPUS'S POWER BY

- Reading Jules Verne's *20,000 Leagues Under the Sea*
- Experimenting with disguises

An octopus avoids predators either by swimming backwards or by discharging a cloud of inky fluid that resembles its shape and acts as a decoy. What creative methods can you use to avoid harmful confrontations in business and daily life?

As a dream symbol
Mother, skilfulness, peripheral vision, freedom, home, emotional intensity

As a guardian or protector
Protects by threatening
Avoids danger by sidestepping the problem

As a healer
Alleviates stomach problems
Heals through emotional release

As an oracle or omen
Be more direct
Watch for attack from the side

CRAB

MYTHS AND STORIES

According to Greek legend, the goddess Hera placed a gigantic crab in the night sky to form the constellation Cancer. The crab is a mother symbol.

IF CRAB IS YOUR POWER ANIMAL

In business, you are able to shift your focus instantaneously and quickly move in a sideways direction to confuse your competitors. You have skill in many areas including cooking, gardening and managing money. When it comes to your own life, you learn your best lessons when the unexpected happens. When feeling moody, you retreat into yourself, go deep and surface when you have uncovered the source of your discontent. That hard shell of yours belies your soft, sensitive nature. But, because of your tough exterior, you flourish in hostile situations where others might wither. You are sensual, intuitive and even sentimental at times. You have to work at knowing when to hold on and when to let go of outworn relationships and possessions.

ASK CRAB TO HELP YOU

- Expand your spiritual awareness
- Heal your relationship with your mother
- Control your negative emotions

ACCESS CRAB'S POWER BY

- Releasing old useless possessions
- Paying attention to your peripheral vision

The astrological sign of Cancer (21 June to 22 July) is symbolized by the crab. Those born under the sign of Cancer are intuitive, artistic and emotional. Are you able to express your emotions freely without embarrassment?

INTERPRETATION GUIDE

As a dream symbol
Dance, camouflage, fragility, magic, healing, gender-bending

As a guardian or protector
Protects with camouflage and disguise
Defends against strong waves

As a healer
Lowers cholesterol
Cures asthma

As an oracle or omen
Be open to magic
Accept your vulnerability

SEAHORSE

MYTHS AND STORIES

Neptune, the Roman god of the sea, is depicted in a chariot drawn by seahorses. In Asia, the seahorse is still thought to have magical and medicinal qualities.

IF SEAHORSE IS YOUR POWER ANIMAL

You are monogamous and marry for life. You love to dance with your spouse and waltz around the room on a daily basis. This might be the key to how you maintain your happy marriage. If you are male you are the one who stays home with the kids. Whether male or female you may seem very cute and innocent, but you are actually very aggressive in getting what you want. Unfortunately, your health is fragile and you suffer from various chronic diseases, such as asthma. Because of this you know better than most how to manage your energy. You are a great mimic and will take on the voice, mannerisms and dress of those around you. Your captivating personality charms everyone you meet. Be careful that life's emotional storms don't tear you away from your somewhat tentative grip on reality.

ASK SEAHORSE TO HELP YOU

- Blend in to stay out of the limelight
- Keep your romantic relationship alive

ACCESS SEAHORSE'S POWER BY

- Raising your own seahorses in a fish tank
- Wearing camouflage clothing

The courtship dance of seahorses is wonderful to watch. The male initiates by pumping up his belly and parading before the female to entice her into dancing. Try learning ballroom dancing or the tango to spice up your romance.

As a dream symbol
Imagination, joy, play, creativity,
sociability, flow, curiosity

As a guardian or protector
Protects during change
Protects from malicious gossip

As a healer
Heals through play
Heals with deep breathing

As an oracle or omen
Separate yourself from
negative people
Release self-imposed limitations

SEAL

MYTHS AND STORIES

Scottish tales tell of *selkies* or sea fairies, who every ninth night would shed their seal skins and dance on the beach as humans.

IF SEAL IS YOUR POWER ANIMAL

You have a playful nature and love spending the day at the beach. You have the uncanny ability to move from anger to complete calm, with no residual hangover. If you have a fight you never hold a grudge. You know how to go with the flow in the ever-changing realities of life. You strive to enjoy this moment because you know, ultimately, that is all there is. Sociable and gregarious, you love to invite friends over for meals. Your active imagination helps you manifest your desires – whether a new outfit or a high-paying job. That playful exterior of yours hides a deeply spiritual person who knows how to listen to his or her inner voice. It is that inner voice that is the source of your wisdom, creativity and balanced approach to life.

ASK SEAL TO HELP YOU

- Use your imagination in all areas of your life
- Flow with whatever life presents

ACCESS SEAL'S POWER BY

- Inviting friends over to play board games
- Watching seals play in the water

Seals have the ability to stay warm in frigid water. If you are feeling a lack of warmth in your life, create your own by making a soothing hot drink and sipping it in front of a roaring fire.

As a dream symbol
Trust, enthusiasm, joy, empathy, curiosity, feminine sensibility, lightness of being

As a guardian or protector
Sustains family
Guards against wastefulness

As a healer
Cures through touch
Heals inner child

As an oracle or omen
Stop worrying
Life is what you make it

SEA OTTER

MYTHS AND STORIES

The Native American Chippewa tribe used otter skin for making medicine bags. The Yup'ik tribe believed the otter could take on human form.

IF SEA OTTER IS YOUR POWER ANIMAL

You are a tremendously curious person. You are not trying to be nosey; you just need to check out everything for yourself. Relaxed and fun-loving, you know how to enjoy life. You are very open and trusting. Your friends love you for this but, for your own safety, you should be a little more circumspect. You are an excellent swimmer, but you really enjoy just playing in the water. Others would do well to emulate the ease with which you negotiate life's difficulties. You know how to nurture and take care of yourself so you make little demand on others. You are a family person, love your kids and adore social events. You love talking with people and will stay up all night trading stories. For you, the future is always bright.

ASK SEA OTTER TO HELP YOU

- Trust your inner wisdom about people and situations
- Greet every day with enthusiasm

ACCESS SEA OTTER'S POWER BY

- Playing on a water slide
- Floating on your back in a pool

A sea otter prises open shellfish by floating on its back, balancing a rock on its belly and hammering the shellfish against it. How can you use your creativity to solve the problems facing you at work or at home?

As a dream symbol
Magician, mysticism, rebirth, death, transformation, awakening, intelligence

As a guardian or protector
Protects by mobbing enemies
Guards home or business

As a healer
Draws out negative energy
Facilitates long-distance healing

As an oracle or omen
Psychological or actual death
Transformation is at hand

RAVEN

MYTHS AND STORIES

In a Welsh legend, the hero Owein used his army of 300 ravens to fight King Arthur.

IF RAVEN IS YOUR POWER ANIMAL

For whatever reason you have an intimate understanding of death. You have given your own passing much thought; yet you are not afraid, because you know there is life after death. You have had many spiritual awakenings and accumulated much wisdom. You have found it exciting and illuminating to discover there are many dimensions to yourself and the universe. A master of unearthing inner demons, you are a great helper and guide for those in need of psychological and spiritual healing. You are a great companion for those exploring the depths of their unconscious. By helping people explore their dark emotions – greed, hatred and jealousy – you help them transform their negativity into wisdom. To strangers you may appear to be a veritable prince of darkness, but underneath those somber black clothes, you are delightful, playful and full of mischief.

ASK RAVEN TO HELP YOU

- Exorcize your inner demons
- Come to terms with death as part of life

ACCESS RAVEN'S POWER BY

- Picking up shiny objects in the grass
- Studying the Mexican Day of the Dead celebration

The poem **'The Raven'**, *written by the American Edgar Allan Poe in 1845, is about the death of his wife. The raven enters the author's home and repeats the word 'nevermore'. Take it as a message to embrace your life fully in this moment.*

INTERPRETATION GUIDE

As a dream symbol
Messenger, vision, war, patience, detachment, authority, spiritual power

As a guardian or protector
Defends through surveillance
Guards against war

As a healer
Heals eye diseases
Cleanses your aura

As an oracle or omen
Strength in battle
Hard times are over

EAGLE

MYTHS AND STORIES

North American Indian headdresses were often made with eagle feathers. The eagle symbolized the Great Spirit, because it flies higher than any other bird.

IF EAGLE IS YOUR POWER ANIMAL

You have a deep connection with a higher power. Others look to you for spiritual guidance. Your startlingly majestic and powerful presence bestows you with a natural authority. Your soaring intelligence inspires your friends, as well as your ability to hear what is in their heart and soul, even if they can't. When friends feel lost, your great clarity of vision helps them see the truth of their situation. You watch what you say and how you say it, because you know you can shred someone to pieces with your words. Because you have such great power, you are very careful not to give in to anger.

You are extraordinarily patient because you know that with patience all things are possible. You forgo judgement and practise kindness, toward yourself and others. Others envy your freedom because, unlike themselves, you are not attached to material possessions.

ASK EAGLE TO HELP YOU
- Practise patience
- Have clear vision in all areas of your life

ACCESS EAGLE'S POWER BY
- Composing your own prayers
- Having your vision tested and corrected

The eagle's eyesight is ten times more powerful than a human's. If you wear glasses or have problems with your eyesight, try eye exercises to strengthen the muscles around your eyes, which will in turn strengthen your vision.

As a dream symbol
Prophetic insight, acute vision, truth, destiny, fearlessness

As a guardian or protector
Protects from unseen danger
Guards against false illusions

As a healer
Heals through internal cleansing
Calms overactive mind

As an oracle or omen
Be observant
Don't overanalyze

HAWK

MYTHS AND STORIES

The Greek goddess Artemis is sometimes depicted with a hawk on her head. In ancient Vedic culture in India, the sun was compared to a hawk circling in the air.

IF HAWK IS YOUR POWER ANIMAL

You know how to pay attention to the subtle messages in your surroundings – an odd tone of voice, a nervous tic, a bird outside your window. When you receive these messages, you immediately look for the underlying truth. Unlike most, your spiritual and material lives are fully integrated. You use your discriminating mind to eliminate anything – a relationship, a job or a bad habit – that does not serve your higher purpose. Others are amazed at your uncanny ability to predict the future. If the situation calls for it, you can swiftly eliminate any adversary with your biting words. You know when you have lost your spiritual vision if you start overanalyzing people or situations.

ASK HAWK TO HELP YOU

- Awaken to the spiritual purpose of your life
- Abandon what hinders your spiritual goals

ACCESS HAWK'S POWER BY

- Writing your spiritual biography
- Consulting an astrologer to predict your future

If the hawk is your power animal, study yoga to release your kundalini energy (see page 8). Kundalini is a Sanskrit word that refers to the spiritual energy that lies sleeping, like a coiled serpent waiting to be released, at the base of your spine.

INTERPRETATION GUIDE

As a dream symbol
Mothering, peace, promise, emotional release, innocence, birth

As a guardian or protector
Sustains warmth of the home
Shelters against abuse

As a healer
Heals with healthy nutrition
Cures through its distinctive cooing sound

As an oracle or omen
Expect a messenger
You need peace and harmony

DOVE

MYTHS AND STORIES

The dove was the companion of the Semitic goddess Astarte. A dove holding an olive branch was a symbol of the Greek goddess Athena.

IF DOVE IS YOUR POWER ANIMAL

Home, security and mothering are extremely important to you. You may have had a difficult childhood and still struggle to create the warmth, protection and security you lacked. In Chinese Medicine, lack of maternal nurturing manifests in problems with digestion and metabolism. Because of your childhood, you may make your living as a professional nutritionist or have a great interest in nutrition. You have a gift when it comes to helping others release emotional trauma or hidden emotions, either from the past or present. This is because you have worked hard to do this yourself. You know that only when inner turmoil is expressed and cleared, can your life open to new possibilities. Your soft, quiet voice is soothing to those around you.

ASK DOVE TO HELP YOU

- Heal emotional trauma from your past
- Create a secure and comfortable home
- Develop nurturing relationships

ACCESS DOVE'S POWER BY

- Eating a diet rich in seeds, nuts and fruit
- Being a peacemaker in a family dispute

Doves lay only two eggs per brood. In numerology, the number two can mean Duality, Division, Polarity, Choice, Balancer of Opposites, Patience, and Positive and Negative. In what ways does the number two manifest in your life, your work and your relationships?

As a dream symbol
Adaptability, trickster, creation, mischief, truth, wit, intelligence

As a guardian or protector
Defends through watchfulness
Ensures the safety of a group

As a healer
Promotes group therapy
Heals through creativity

As an oracle or omen
You will be taking a journey
Danger is nearby

CROW

MYTHS AND STORIES

For Native Americans, the crow knew the deep mysteries of life. Many cultures believe the cawing of crows tells of a coming storm.

IF CROW IS YOUR POWER ANIMAL

Never shy, you are the first to speak up in a meeting or at a dinner. Although not really dishonest, you can be sly and deceptive. A bit of a trickster, you will give false impressions to confuse others. Nothing escapes your keen intelligence. You have a tight group of friends and will get into mischief wherever you go. You learn from each other's explorations, seek each other's advice on who to marry or what car to buy. You are so close it is almost as if you have a secret language. When people speak you have the uncanny ability to hear the truth of what is being said. You are intriguing to strangers, but they soon find you irritating because you flaunt your intelligence. You love divination and may be good at reading the Tarot or Runes.

ASK CROW TO HELP YOU

- Remedy your loneliness and make more friends
- Discover that life is magical and full of potential

ACCESS CROW'S POWER BY

- Starting a club or support group
- Creating an exciting game

The crow is black, which symbolizes potential. *Black is not a colour; rather, it is the absence of colour. It is also mysterious, providing a sense of possibility. What gifts have you been given that you have not yet developed?*

INTERPRETATION GUIDE

As a dream symbol
Darkness, spirits, mystery, magic, astral projection, secrets

As a guardian or protector
Protects with acute hearing
Guards at dawn and dusk

As a healer
Heals indigestion
Improves night vision

As an oracle or omen
Keep silent
Embrace darkness without fear

OWL

MYTHS AND STORIES

The owl was sacred to the Greek goddess Athena and was a symbol of wisdom. The Ainu of Japan called the owl 'beloved deity'.

IF OWL IS YOUR POWER ANIMAL

You are a private complex person and you rarely like others to know what you are thinking. This withholding aspect of your personality can sometimes lead to difficulty and misunderstanding with friends, co-workers or romantic partners. You have many quirky abilities that set you apart from others. For example, you can slip in and out of places quietly. You could be a detective or a spy, but you are most likely a therapist or counsellor. Others remark that your large eyes give you a wise appearance, but sometimes they feel you are staring through them. You have great night vision and exceptional hearing abilities. Because of this, you can also hear what is not being said and see what is hidden in the shadows of the heart. Your gifts can help others work through their emotional pain.

ASK OWL TO HELP YOU

- Be more open in your relationships
- Use your gifts to help others

ACCESS OWL'S POWER BY

- Sitting outdoors at night and listening to the sounds
- Using your wisdom and insight to solve problems

The owl has a third eyelid that moves from side to side cleansing the eye and clearing vision. The ability to see truth depends on the willingness to see and accept things as they are, rather than how you want them to be.

ROOSTER

MYTHS AND STORIES

The Greek god Hermes had a chariot drawn by roosters. The cock or rooster was sacred to the Celtic goddess Brigit and is a symbol of sexuality.

IF ROOSTER IS YOUR POWER ANIMAL

Maybe you have accomplished something and you want others to take note and that's why you are 'crowing'. Or, perhaps you are strutting around showing off your new flashy outfit. You are a cocky, confident, hardworking person and always the optimist. Your direct approach to life is refreshing in a world where manipulation is the name of the game. Even though your antics can be annoying, your friends have great affection for you. For your co-workers who drag themselves into the office every day, morning would not be the same without your energetic and cheerful greeting. You also have a more serious side, which you rarely show in public – your love of things of the spirit and your devotion to your chosen religion. You are always vigilant for the presence of negativity or sin in yourself and others.

ASK ROOSTER TO HELP YOU

- Create a shield of psychic protection to warn of danger
- Physically protect your spouse and family

ACCESS ROOSTER'S POWER BY

- Reading a book on how to have great sex
- Having supreme confidence in yourself

The rooster crows heralding a new dawn. Most of its crowing takes place in the early morning, because that is when it is most vocal about protecting its territory. Are you protecting your boundaries from those who would violate them?

INTERPRETATION GUIDE

As a dream symbol
Balance, grace, agility, solitude, insight, dignity, self-confidence

As a guardian or protector
Protects against insecurity
Warns against self-absorption

As a healer
Heals physical balance
Promotes stillness and quiet

As an oracle or omen
Follow your own path
Career opportunity

HERON

MYTHS AND STORIES

In Egypt, the heron was associated with the gods Osiris and Bennu.

IF HERON IS YOUR POWER ANIMAL

Others will catch you standing alone, motionless and in deep thought. They admire your ability to be so self-contained and emotionally balanced. Whatever's going on around you – friends making demands, traffic jams – you always honour your own personal rhythm. You have a strong emotional nature. In work, you combine your deeply held feelings and your passion with your considerable ambition to accomplish your goals. Although not selfish you know how to take advantage of situations for your own benefit. Solitary and independent you are a person who enjoys your own company. You avoid 9 to 5 jobs and prefer to experiment with many different kinds of work. You radiate a silent power and elegant grace and embody both emotional and physical balance. That exquisite balance is the gift you offer the world.

ASK HERON TO HELP YOU

- Learn to focus and meditate
- Eliminate any sense of self-pity
- Strike when opportunity presents itself

ACCESS HERON'S POWER BY

- Wading in a shallow pond or lake
- Doing something you have never done before

The heron will appear to be asleep, then make a lightning move, catching its victim in its long bill. Are you prepared to respond quickly when a business opportunity appears or a new job is advertised that you would like?

INTERPRETATION GUIDE

As a dream symbol
Scavenging, ecology, communication, messenger, freedom, enjoyment, empathy

As a guardian or protector
Defends the perimeter of your property
Protects through good communication

As a healer
Supports authentic lifestyles
Heals poor appetite

As an oracle or omen
Address a difficult problem
Stay above conflict

SEAGULL

MYTHS AND STORIES

The ancient Celts considered the seagull to be a messenger from the Otherworld.

IF SEAGULL IS YOUR POWER ANIMAL

You tend to bob on the surface of life, avoid worry and go with the flow. The in-between world of the shoreline, neither sea nor land, appeals to you. You could be a bartender or a beach bum or run a successful business for tourists. Your more conservative family members worry about your relaxed and easygoing attitude. Your untidy appearance, your casual approach to where you live and your poor housekeeping skills, embarrass them. That said, many pasty-skinned office workers secretly envy your unorthodox lifestyle. When it comes to relationships you are always kind and fair in your dealings with others. Although you are light-hearted, your emotions run deep, making you an empathetic listener. You are an excellent communicator and can interpret subtle body language. You have a strong spiritual life and are very comfortable praying.

ASK SEAGULL TO HELP YOU

- Relax and enjoy the good things of life
- Be more open to unorthodox lifestyles

ACCESS SEAGULL'S POWER BY

- Spending a day collecting seashells
- Learning about or taking a ride on a seaplane

In America, the residents of Salt Lake City, Utah, erected a monument to the seagulls that consumed millions of grasshoppers in 1848, saving the settlers' crops. Express gratitude to anyone who has rescued or saved you from disaster in your lifetime.

As a dream symbol
Poetry, mysticism, song, beauty, grace, eroticism, elegance

As a guardian or protector
Sustains with strong arms
Warns against reactivity

As a healer
Promotes longevity
Encourages tranquillity

As an oracle or omen
Expect an erotic encounter
Read poetry

SWAN

MYTHS AND STORIES

In Greek myth, the god Zeus disguises himself as a swan to seduce the goddess Leda. The result of their passion is the World Egg.

IF SWAN IS YOUR POWER ANIMAL

Graceful and elegant, you seem to glide through life leaving hardly a ripple in your wake. Others learn from your tranquil personality how to reduce conflict and maintain their serenity. When it is called for, you have the ability to move very fast. You know how to manage energy and reach goals with speed and efficiency. This gives you the endurance to complete long projects – from creating a new product line, to running a marathon. You are a devoted partner and uphold commitments in all areas of your life. You know how to see the inner beauty in everyone regardless of outward appearance.

You have strong erotic desires and consider your sexual life to be sacred. Poetry books line your shelves and you also love to sing.

ASK SWAN TO HELP YOU

- Awaken to your power and inner beauty
- Negotiate difficult situations without causing negativity
- Get in touch with your erotic desires

ACCESS SWAN'S POWER BY

- Watching swans swim for an hour
- Improving your posture and comportment
- Telling your partner a sexual secret

Swans have strong family ties. They mate for life and the young may remain with their parents until they find their own mate. Keep your family relationships strong by practising open and honest communication and unconditional love.

As a dream symbol
Creativity, storytelling, safe return, beginnings, marriage, fidelity

As a guardian or protector
Guards territory
Defends the young

As a healer
Cures fear of flying
Promotes couples' counselling

As an oracle or omen
Expect good news
Embark on a spiritual quest

GOOSE

MYTHS AND STORIES

Aphrodite, the Greek goddess of love, is depicted riding a goose. The Indian goddess Devi, the inventor of the alphabet, is sometimes shown riding a goose. The goose is associated with creativity and storytelling.

IF GOOSE IS YOUR POWER ANIMAL

You are a faithful and loving marriage partner. You value the comfort and safety of your home life. You love storytelling and when your extended family gets together, you love to tell family stories. You may also spin tall tales in order to deliver subtle messages to those listening. On your off time, you are usually working on a novel or screenplay. You have probably logged more frequent flyer miles than most of your friends combined, because you love to travel. Yearly family vacations inspire and renew your creative life. You work well in a team, but always keep your personal vision clear and intact. You are mostly even-tempered but when you are angered you will bite hard.

ASK GOOSE TO HELP YOU

- Express yourself through writing
- Break free of childhood fears that are holding you back

ACCESS GOOSE'S POWER BY

- Buying or making a goose quill pen
- Writing a short story
- Reading favourite stories from your childhood

Graceful in flight, the goose has great endurance during migrations, flying up to 1,600 km (1,000 miles) without stopping. Build up your own ability to endure life's hardships by eating well, getting enough rest and having a strong spiritual life.

As a dream symbol
Birth, children, fidelity, home, luck,
dance, parenting

As a guardian or protector
Protects newborns
Guards against miscarriages

As a healer
Supports a healthy pregnancy
Promotes dance therapy

As an oracle or omen
Nurture your creative projects
Explore dance

STORK

MYTHS AND STORIES

The stork is sacred to the Roman goddess
Juno, the protector of the home, children
and family.

IF STORK IS YOUR POWER ANIMAL

You have a tremendous interest in the
welfare of children. You not only have, or
want, your own kids, but you may have a job
that brings you close to children – a teacher,
childcare worker, paediatrician or child
advocate. Whether male or female you know
the importance of giving birth in one's life,
whether it is giving birth to children, to ideas
or to creative endeavours. Your other major
interest is dance. For you, dance is a sacred
activity. When you dance, you not only have
fun, you access your deepest emotions.
When you are troubled you don't spend
time thinking. You prefer to find the answer
to your problems through movement and
the wisdom of your body. Through your
body and your emotions you inform your
mind. You also use dance to commune
with the Divine.

ASK STORK TO HELP YOU

- Return home to heal old wounds
- Be a better parent or parent figure

ACCESS STORK'S POWER BY

- Rearranging your own 'nest' to make it
  more comfortable for your family
- Taking a dance class

*The legend that new babies are brought to the
home by a stork arises from the fact that this bird
takes loving care of its own young. If you have
children in your life, listen to and honour their
needs and concerns.*

As a dream symbol
Voice, good fortune, self-defence,
longevity, spirit, grace, flexibility

As a guardian or protector
Defends with a powerful yell
Protects using martial arts

As a healer
Heals though releasing the voice
Develops longevity

As an oracle or omen
Do not divide your attention
Good fortune

CRANE

MYTHS AND STORIES

In Oriental cultures the crane symbolizes good fortune and longevity.

IF CRANE IS YOUR POWER ANIMAL

You understand the importance of the voice. You may take voice lessons of all kinds, including singing, public speaking and therapeutic chanting or vocalizing. You know the power of accessing one's primal voice in healing emotional trauma. Sometimes you roll up the car windows and let out a long, harsh and penetrating yell. The vibrations clear your head and release stuck emotions. Using your voice in this way gets you in touch with your own truth. You also study Chinese martial arts to enhance your physical health, emotional stability and mental clarity. You are skilled at self-defence but your main focus is self-development. When things are not going well in life you have the wisdom to try a different approach to achieving your goals. You are a dedicated spiritual practitioner and believe in the potential of enlightenment.

ASK CRANE TO HELP YOU

- Release the power of your voice
- Learn to defend yourself without becoming aggressive

ACCESS CRANE'S POWER BY

- Taking a martial arts class
- Learning a spiritual chant

The whooping crane, the rarest of all cranes, has a call that can be heard up to 3 km (2 miles) away. If you feel your voice is constricted in any way, consider taking voice lessons to release your physical and emotional voice.

As a dream symbol
War, thunder, prophecy, drumming,
rhythm, hidden layers, unconventionality

As a guardian or protector
Guards your territory
Defends unconventional lifestyles

As a healer
Alleviates neck problems
Promotes deep systemic healing

As an oracle or omen
A storm is approaching
Use your head

WOODPECKER

MYTHS AND STORIES

The Romans associated the woodpecker with Mars, the god of war and the Greeks with Zeus, the god of thunder. Native Americans thought the woodpecker drew thunder from the sky with its drumming.

IF WOODPECKER IS YOUR POWER ANIMAL

You loved climbing trees as a kid and you may now enjoy hiking and mountain climbing. Flexible and nimble, others find it hard to catch up with you. You have a unique way of navigating the world and definitely march to your own drum. You validate your own rhythms which may be reflected in your unconventional lifestyle. Because you are so independent you are a bit territorial and controlling about your space and your possessions. You are quite lovable, so your friends and family are willing to struggle with you over this issue. They admire your perseverance in pursuing your dreams and your ability to bore into a problem or personal issue until you find the truth.

ASK WOODPECKER TO HELP YOU

• Forge your own path
• Be more flexible and less controlling

ACCESS WOODPECKER'S POWER BY

• Wearing black and white clothes and a red cap or hat
• Joining a drumming circle

The majestic American ivory-billed woodpecker, long believed to be extinct, was recently rediscovered in an Arkansas wildlife area. What part of you do you feel has become extinct? Have you lost your childhood playfulness or your sense of adventure?

As a dream symbol
Beauty, manoeuvrability, sweetness, joy,
perseverance, endurance, wonder

As a guardian or protector
Protects by divebombing
Defends the young

As a healer
Corrects blood sugar imbalance
Promotes good metabolism

As an oracle or omen
Enjoy life
Conserve your energy

HUMMINGBIRD

MYTHS AND STORIES

The South American Aztec god Quetzalcoatl,
was depicted as a serpent wearing iridescent
hummingbird feathers.

IF HUMMINGBIRD IS YOUR
POWER ANIMAL

You wear striking, colourful clothes. If male, you
are a charming suitor who seduces your lover
and then leaves her in the lurch. Whether male
or female, you are very energetic and can go
the distance when others give up or fail. You
are extremely productive and complete
projects ahead of time. Your versatility is
reflected in your resumé that lists your many
diverse skills. Your energetic personality attracts
employers, so you have no problem finding
work that you enjoy. When there is a problem,
you are the one who sees it from all angles,
finding the best solution for everyone involved.

You expend so much energy you have to be
careful to eat well and watch your sugar
intake. If you need to confront a weakness,
such as an addiction, you have the courage
to do so.

ASK HUMMINGBIRD TO HELP YOU

- Analyze problems from many angles
- Increase your productivity

ACCESS HUMMINGBIRD'S POWER BY

- Buying a hummingbird feeder to attract
  hummingbirds
- Wearing something iridescent

*The ruby-throated hummingbird, weighing only 3 g
(⅛ oz), migrates 3,000 km (1,800 miles) from the
eastern USA to winter in Central America. Don't
underestimate your ability to achieve your dreams
and accomplish what you want to in this lifetime.*

INTERPRETATION GUIDE

As a dream symbol
Transformation, fragility, joy,
clairvoyance, metamorphosis, beauty,
summer

As a guardian or protector
Shelters during transitions
Guards against flightiness

As a healer
Heals the spirit
Transforms delusions into wisdom

As an oracle or omen
Expect more joy
A wedding is imminent

BUTTERFLY

MYTHS AND STORIES

Ancient Mexicans dedicated an entire palace to the butterfly at Teotihuacan. For the Haida Indians of the Pacific Northwest, the Raven was considered the creator of the world and the butterfly the raven's spokesperson.

IF BUTTERFLY IS YOUR POWER ANIMAL

Your heightened sensitivity may give you clairvoyant abilities. You have strong spiritual goals and keep them in focus at all times. In times past, you may have had difficulties – perhaps a troubled childhood, psychological problems or a failed marriage. But you have emerged, after a time of hard work and introspection, into the joyful person you are today. You have the wisdom and experience to recognize when others are in a process of transformation and at what stage they are in their journey. Most find you charming and you are successful in business and love. You are sensitive to poor air quality and chemical pollutants.

ASK BUTTERFLY TO HELP YOU

- Incubate and protect a creative idea
- Know when you need to withdraw during a transition

ACCESS BUTTERFLY'S POWER BY

- Studying the four stages of the life cycle of a butterfly: egg, caterpillar, pupa and adult
- Learning ways to attract butterflies to your garden

Millions of overlapping scales give butterfly wings their colour and patterns. Iridescent hues come from faceted scales that refract light; solid colours are from pigmented scales. Experiment with the power of colour to change your mood and emotions.

INTERPRETATION GUIDE

As a dream symbol
Manoeuvrability, illusion, mysticism,
swiftness, gentleness, beauty, luminance

As a guardian or protector
Protects children
Prevents rigid thinking

As a healer
Promotes excellent vision
Heals problems with overeating

As an oracle or omen
Change what needs changing
Spend time in the sun

DRAGONFLY

MYTHS AND STORIES

The dragonfly is the national emblem of
Japan, also called the Island of the Dragonfly.
Native American legend holds that the
dragonfly was once actually a dragon.

IF DRAGONFLY IS YOUR POWER ANIMAL

You are an expert at what you do because
you have honed your skill through repetition,
discipline and attention to detail. You are very
emotional and feel things deeply. You respond
to life passionately. Since you have had to work
to control your emotions, you understand
others who struggle with theirs, which makes
you an excellent counsellor or therapist. You
can see through the illusions and limitations of
physical existence. You know life is not what it
appears to be. Because you see situations from
many different angles, you can find solutions to
problems that may elude others.

ASK DRAGONFLY TO HELP YOU

- Be more organized, disciplined and
  efficient in your work
- Balance your mind and emotions
  through meditation
- Be more conscious of the healing
  power of light

ACCESS DRAGONFLY'S POWER BY

- Installing a water feature in your garden
  to attract dragonflies
- Wearing iridescent jewellery or clothing

Dragonflies begin their lives as larvae on the
bottom of streams or ponds and through
metamorphosis become creatures of the air. In
what ways would you like to transform your life
over the next five, ten or 20 years?

As a dream symbol
Industry, prosperity, purity, sexuality,
fertility, pollination, productivity

As a guardian or protector
Defends the soul
Ensures purity

As a healer
Bee sting therapy may help arthritis
Prevents infection

As an oracle or omen
Pursue your dreams
Get busy

BEE

MYTHS AND STORIES

The Hindu gods Vishnu, Krishna and Indra are all associated with the bee. The bee was also sacred in Greece. The goddess Demeter was considered the 'Queen Bee' and her human priestesses were called the 'bees'.

IF BEE IS YOUR POWER ANIMAL

You are a team player and a diligent worker. You live for your family and community. Because your identity is so tied to them if you are away for any reason you will feel disoriented. You don't mind taking orders and are happiest when you are doing a good job. It is difficult for you to balance work and leisure. You have to remind yourself to stop and enjoy the sweetness of life. Most experience you as radiating sensual and sexual energy. You have a fertile mind, full of ideas and projects.

ASK BEE TO HELP YOU

- Be more productive in your work
- Accomplish anything that appears to be impossible

ACCESS BEE'S POWER BY

- Visiting a beehive and learning about bees and beekeeping
- Eating raw organic honey

Queen bees consume Royal Jelly as their only food, while worker bees eat Royal Jelly only briefly after birth. As a result, the queen bee is 40–60% larger and lives 40% longer than worker bees. The nutrients in Royal Jelly are also said to be beneficial for the human body.

INTERPRETATION GUIDE

As a dream symbol
Magic, discernment, charisma, colour, mimicry, speech, beauty, sun

As a guardian or protector
Protects using loud voice
Guards against malicious gossip

As a healer
Cures depression
Heals using colour light therapy

As an oracle or omen
Think before you speak
Don't fall for flattery

PARROT

MYTHS AND STORIES

One of the four sacred clans of the Hopi Indians is the Parrot clan. The Hindu god of love, Kama, is associated with the parrot.

IF PARROT IS YOUR POWER ANIMAL

You are an alert, highly intelligent, curious person who enjoys the company of family and friends. You are a talker and will rattle on chatting and telling stories into the night. But you also know when to be quiet and listen. Because of your ability to be highly entertaining as well as empathetic, you have a lot of friends. You are always the one everyone knows at a party, even if they don't know each other. You are the link among your different groups of friends. Colourful and charismatic, you uplift everyone around you, giving them a sense of hope and promise for the future. You generate

excitement and a sense that everything and anything is possible.

ASK PARROT TO HELP YOU

- Rediscover your dreams and work toward realizing them
- Value and spend more time with your family and friends

ACCESS PARROT'S POWER BY

- Dressing in striking colours that make you look exceptionally beautiful
- Trying colour therapy or chromotherapy

The grey parrot has been shown to use human words to communicate feelings such as hunger, fear or boredom. How well do you communicate your feelings to others? Do you always know what you are feeling?

INTERPRETATION GUIDE

As a dream symbol
Vanity, royalty, dignity, beauty, self-confidence, warning

As a guardian or protector
Warns of intruders
Sustains your aura or energy field

As a healer
Heals through foot reflexology
Corrects vision problems

As an oracle or omen
Watch out for the evil eye
You will be lucky in love

PEACOCK

MYTHS AND STORIES

In ancient Egypt, the peacock was shown as a companion of the goddess Isis. In ancient China, Japan, Babylon and Persia the peacock was a symbol of royalty.

IF PEACOCK IS YOUR POWER ANIMAL

You are self-confident. You have the ability to see into the future and can teach others how to become clairvoyant. You are highly sensitive and have to work to protect your personal energy field. You are dignified and regal in your bearing and appearance. At the top of your chosen field, you enjoy the recognition and praise bestowed on you. One might imagine you to be arrogant, but in reality you don't take all this too seriously. You know it can all be gone in the blink of an eye. Instead, you try to enjoy life as best you can.

ASK PEACOCK TO HELP YOU

- Remember to laugh at life, especially when things are not going well
- Put yourself forward in the world and believe in yourself

ACCESS PEACOCK'S POWER BY

- Wearing bright, iridescent colours
- Reciting affirmations for self-esteem on a daily basis

The male peacock's feathers *grow from its back and not its tail. During courtship, it spreads its train into a gorgeous iridescent blue/green fan with eye-shaped markings. Allow yourself to dress more beautifully in order to honour your sacred nature.*

As a dream symbol
Transformation, renewal, night, rebirth, initiation, adaptation

As a guardian or protector
Protects from collision
Guards during the night

As a healer
Brings good luck and happiness
Alleviates ear and hearing problems

As an oracle or omen
Watch for hidden opportunities
Follow bat's example of hanging upside down and try inverted yoga postures

BAT

MYTHS AND STORIES

The bat was sacred to the Native American Aztec, Toltec and Mayan people as a symbol of rebirth. In China, the bat was associated with Show-Hsing, the god of longevity.

IF BAT IS YOUR POWER ANIMAL

Because you have honed your psychic skills, you have an extraordinary ability to comprehend the hidden messages in any situation. When life presents difficulties, such as a loss of your job or a serious illness, you will adapt to the new situation, regroup and regenerate your life force. If, however, you lose your spiritual moorings, you will become confused and stumble. You understand the need to confront your ego, a major obstacle that prevents your spiritual growth. You have been through many transformations that have turned your ordinary perceptions upside down. Each one has felt like a mini death and rebirth, which resulted in new realizations about your true purpose on Earth.

ASK BAT TO HELP YOU

- Uncover hidden messages
- Recognize opportunities and gifts

ACCESS BAT'S POWER BY

- Being active at dusk and after dark
- Installing a bat house in your garden for controlling insects

Bats navigate by means of short, high-frequency sounds that they make continually while flying. From these echoes, the animals can determine the direction and distance of objects in the area. Work to become more present in the moment by developing your senses.

INTERPRETATION GUIDE

As a dream symbol
Wisdom, healing, protection, paradox, stamina, determination

As a guardian or protector
Defends against poisonous snakes
Warns against dualistic thinking

As a healer
Heals kidney diseases
Removes cancer-causing toxins

As an oracle or omen
Move beyond conventional reality
Root out poisons

GARUDA

MYTHS AND STORIES

The garuda is a mythical creature, half-human, half-bird, sacred to Buddhist and Hindu traditions. It symbolizes humans as half-animal, half-spiritual beings, capable of moving between different dimensions.

IF GARUDA IS YOUR POWER ANIMAL

You are a powerful spiritual practitioner devoted to your spiritual path. You have the wisdom to embrace paradox, which is the capacity to stand the tension and anxiety that may emerge when things that are opposite or contradictory are both true. For example, a person may have the capacity for great kindness and frightening cruelty. You can accept his or her complex nature with compassion, without praising or condemning. You do not fall for a rigid, dualistic, black and white view of life. You are embodied and human, yet know that God or Buddha nature resides within you. When poisonous situations appear in your life you will immediately strike to remove them.

ASK GARUDA TO HELP YOU

- Remove anything toxic in your life
- Embrace your spiritual nature and destiny

ACCESS GARUDA'S POWER BY

- Studying the garuda in Hindu and Buddhist mythology
- Meditating on images of the garuda in Hindu and Buddhist art

In Buddhism, the garuda is considered to remove disease caused by poisons. The worst poisons are desire, hatred and ignorance. Monitor your mind for thoughts that are influenced by these three poisons, and replace them with non-attachment, love and wisdom.

As a dream symbol
Strength, intelligence, vision, courage, majesty, vengeance, salvation

As a guardian or protector
Protects treasure
Guards Tree of Knowledge

As a healer
Heals blindness
Cures from poisoning

As an oracle or omen
Combine intelligence and strength
Be open to magic and mystery

GRIFFIN

MYTHS AND STORIES

The griffin is a magical creature with the face, talons and wings of an eagle and the body of a lion. The griffin represented Apollo, the Greek god of strength and Nemesis, the goddess of retribution. A major heraldic animal, it has been emblazoned on the shields of knights and forms the coat of arms of royalty.

IF GRIFFIN IS YOUR POWER ANIMAL

You possess penetrating intelligence and vision. You can unmask deception of all kinds. Others may see you as a hero, perhaps because you once risked your life to pull someone from a car wreck or saved someone from drowning. Whether male or female, you have a strong protective instinct, almost a hypervigilance, especially when guarding against theft. You may even work in law enforcement or the judicial system, as you are keenly interested in the concepts of justice and responsibility for one's actions. You have a powerful, imposing, almost majestic appearance and others are somewhat intimidated by you.

ASK GRIFFIN TO HELP YOU

• Protect those nearest and dearest to you
• Temper your desire to seek revenge when harmed

ACCESS GRIFFIN'S POWER BY

• Learning about the griffin in legend
• Imagining that you are a griffin

As the story goes, there was a great cache of gold in Scythia, a country far to the northeast of Greece. The griffins guarded the gold from those who would steal it. What treasure do you need to guard and protect in your life?

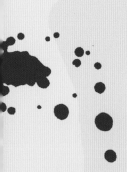

As a dream symbol
Resurrection, immortality, life after death, rising sun, hope, transformation

As a guardian or protector
Shelters from despair
Defends the heart

As a healer
Heals traumatic experiences
Heals blindness

As an oracle or omen
You will be reborn
Important events to come

PHOENIX

MYTHS AND STORIES

When the phoenix has lived for 500 years, it builds itself a nest made of cinnamon twigs in an oak or palm tree and ignites it with the help of the sun. The phoenix and its nest burn furiously and are reduced to ashes, from which a new, young phoenix arises.

IF PHOENIX IS YOUR POWER ANIMAL

You are always scanning the horizon, collecting information about your environment and the events happening around you. A picture of power and grace, you look especially stunning when you wear the colour purple or crimson. You are a person of great courage and high moral values. You have endured terrible misfortune, perhaps a serious illness such as cancer or seeing your home burned to the ground. Even though you were devastated physically and emotionally, you rose from the ashes to renew your life. You are keenly aware of cycles – the moon's phases, the rising and setting of the sun and change of seasons. You give hope and inspiration to those around you.

ASK PHOENIX TO HELP YOU

• Overcome a serious illness or tragedy
• See the larger picture in any situation

ACCESS PHOENIX'S POWER BY

• Burning cinnamon or myrrh incense
• Paying attention to the cycles of time

If your power animal is the phoenix, study the Western zodiac sign Scorpio, the sign of transformation. When you want to transform your negativity, don't try to destroy it, but rather accept it and work to neutralize its effect.

As a dream symbol
Fame, power, gentleness, prosperity,
purity, wisdom

As a guardian or protector
Protects young girls
Guards virginity

As a healer
Heals stomach problems
Cures epilepsy

As an oracle or omen
Success is within your reach
Good times are on the way

UNICORN

MYTHS AND STORIES

The unicorn is a magical white horse with blue eyes, a single spiralling horn on its forehead and cloven hooves. It has been popular since ancient times in both the West and the Orient. In early Christian legends, the unicorn was as small as a goat and very difficult to capture or observe. Many medieval paintings and tapestries depict images of these animals.

IF UNICORN IS YOUR POWER ANIMAL

You have a beautiful mysterious presence. You are a gentle, solitary being, but you will become a fierce warrior if young girls are in need of protection. Although not a doctor, you are knowledgeable about herbal remedies for neutralizing toxins and poison. You are chaste in love and faithful in marriage. You are virtuous in all ways, but your guileless nature leads others to try to take advantage of you. Your purity and virtue are a breath of fresh air in our modern-day corrupt and jaded world.

ASK UNICORN TO HELP YOU

- Maintain your integrity at all times
- Be open to magic and mystery

ACCESS UNICORN'S POWER BY

- Volunteering to help troubled children and young people
- Studying the famous early 16th-century French unicorn tapestries

---

Legend has it that the only way to catch a unicorn is to send a maiden alone into the forest. When the unicorn finds the maiden, he will rest his head in her lap and fall asleep. How can you attract what you want into your life?

INTERPRETATION GUIDE

As a dream symbol
Power, good fortune, change,
transformation, protection,
sexual potency

As a guardian or protector
Maintains wealth or treasure
Wards off evil spirits

As a healer
Insures good hydration
Promotes yogic breath work

As an oracle or omen
Expect to find treasure
Good luck is on the way

DRAGON

MYTHS AND STORIES

The dragon is an immensely powerful magical beast with a serpentine, reptilian body, with legs, wings and fiery breath. In Europe, dragons are portrayed as ferocious, evil beasts that are fought by human beings. But Asian dragons, the wingless variety, are generally considered as friendly creatures that ensure good luck and wealth.

IF DRAGON IS YOUR POWER ANIMAL

You are an extremely powerful person, both physically and mentally. In your untamed state you exhibit greed, hubris and base sexual behaviour. When you transform your negativity you are loved for your fearlessness, warmth and genuineness. You help others overcome their obstacles in life. Always energetic and powerful, you can also be very gentle and playful. Your friends and family greatly appreciate your boundless energy, your generosity and your elegance and class, so much so that they put up with your perfectionism and eccentricity.

ASK DRAGON TO HELP YOU

- Transform your negative habits into healthy ones
- Use your power for good

ACCESS DRAGON'S POWER BY

- Watching a Chinese dragon dance at a Lunar New Year's Day parade
- Viewing images of dragons in world art

In China, on New Year's Day, a group of people will wind through the streets wearing a large dragon costume to scare away evil spirits from spoiling the new year. Create a ritual or prayer to ward off evil spirits from spoiling your own life.

As a dream symbol
Initiation, silence, mysteries,
destruction, knowledge, transition

As a guardian or protector
Guards entries
Defends sacred space

As a healer
Heals through silent retreat
Promotes healing through storytelling

As an oracle or omen
Beware of destructive forces
Keep silent

SPHINX

MYTHS AND STORIES

The sphinx is the most mysterious of magical beings. In Greek mythology, the sphinx was depicted with the body of a lion, the wings of an eagle and the head and breasts of a woman. The Egyptian sphinx has the head of a man and the body, feet and tail of a lion.

IF SPHINX IS YOUR POWER ANIMAL

Most think of you as eccentric. You are quiet and spend much of your time alone studying philosophy and world religions. Friends who know you try to engage you in conversation, wanting to pick your brain about the mysteries of life, but more often than not you decline. Instead, you entertain them with riddles. One of your favourites is as follows. What has one voice and becomes four-footed, two-footed and three-footed? The answer is human beings, who crawl on all fours as a baby, then walk on two legs and finally need a cane in old age.

ASK SPHINX TO HELP YOU

- Understand the great mysteries of life
- Be more aware of what you say when you are speaking

ACCESS SPHINX'S POWER BY

- Studying the Greek and Egyptian sphinxes
- Remaining silent for 24 hours

The largest and oldest sphinx is found near Giza, Egypt. It is 73 m (240 ft) long and 20 m (66 ft) high. The great sphinx has kept its silent watch for 4,500 years. Are you able to maintain your silence when a friend entrusts you with a secret?

INDEX

ACKNOWLEDGEMENTS

Executive Editors Brenda Rosen, Sandra Rigby

Editor Kate Tuckett

Executive Art Editor Sally Bond

Designer Annika Skoog & Pia Ingham for Cobalt Id

Illustrator Brian Grimwood

Production Controller Simone Nauerth

PERSONAL
POWER ANIMALS

For Guidance, Protection and Healing

MADONNA GAUDING